Pr s

Another Exclusive!
Featured on page 11 of our catalog.

Collier Books
Macmillan Publishing Company
New York
Maxwell Macmillan Canada
Toronto
Maxwell Macmillan International
New York Oxford Singapore Sydney

Collier Books
Macmillan Publishing Company
866 Third Avenue
New York, NY 10022

Maxwell Macmillan Canada, Inc.
1200 Eglinton Avenue East
Suite 200
Don Mills, Ontario M3C 3N1

Macmillan Publishing Company is part of the Maxwell Communication Group of Companies.

ISBN 0-02-040291-0

Library of Congress Catalog Card Number 92-34350

Macmillan books are available at special discounts for bulk purchases for sales promotions, premiums, fund-raising, or educational use.
For details, contact:
Special Sales Director
Macmillan Publishing Company
866 Third Avenue
New York, NY 10022

First Collier Books Edition 1993

10 9 8 7 6 5 4 3 2 1

Printed in the United States of America

Other humor books by becker&mayer!

Armchair Golf

Good Dog, Millie

Where's Dan Quayle?

Where's Charles & Di?

The Official Book of Thumb Wrestling

The Supreme Court Cut-Out & Dress-Up Book

GIFTS OVER $5,000

Free gift-wrap!

3-2-1 blast off.

Literally *thousands* of injuries are caused yearly from falling champagne corks. That's why The Cutting Edge teamed up with a consortium of major defense contractors to develop Cork Orbiter™.

Using the latest Space Shuttle aerodynamics and a solid rocket booster powered by nitroglycerine, Cork Orbiter™ develops 100,000 pounds of thrust to lift your cork up, up, and away. Far, far away. For good.

After only three minutes following launch, your champagne cork achieves a perfectly harmless geosynchronous, near-Earth orbit. If, at any time, a malfunction occurs, self-destruct sequences are invoked to assure a safe evening for you and your guests.

When it comes to *your* safety, The Cutting Edge spares no expense. Nor should you.

- **Cork Orbiter™**
  #BOOZUP **$5,499.95 (4.00)**

Is $100,000 too much for a pair of sunglasses? We don't think so.

Just one look at Reality Adjusters™ tells you this is no ordinary pair of sunglasses. Reality Adjusters™ go a step beyond simple UV protection—these sunglasses provide protection from *reality*.

A kinder, gentler reality.

When you slip on a pair of these revolutionary sunglasses, they go right to work—scanning for unwanted images, matching each and every image against its data bank of over ten million digitized images. When a "bad" image is encountered, Reality Adjusters™ will either alter this image or remove it altogether. As a safety precaution, when images are removed or substantially altered, a small red light will flash in the upper right-hand corner of your sunglasses indicating this "reality adjustment."

We have spared no expense in bringing you the finest pair of sunglasses available today. But let's face it—getting or giving the best sometimes costs a few dollars more.

If theft is a problem in your reality, be sure to order the optional alarm system.

- **Reality Adjusters™** #GETREAL **$99,995.95 (50.00)**
- **Alarm System** #GOTTAHVIT **$195.95 (15.00)**

Quite possibly the last watch you'll ever own.

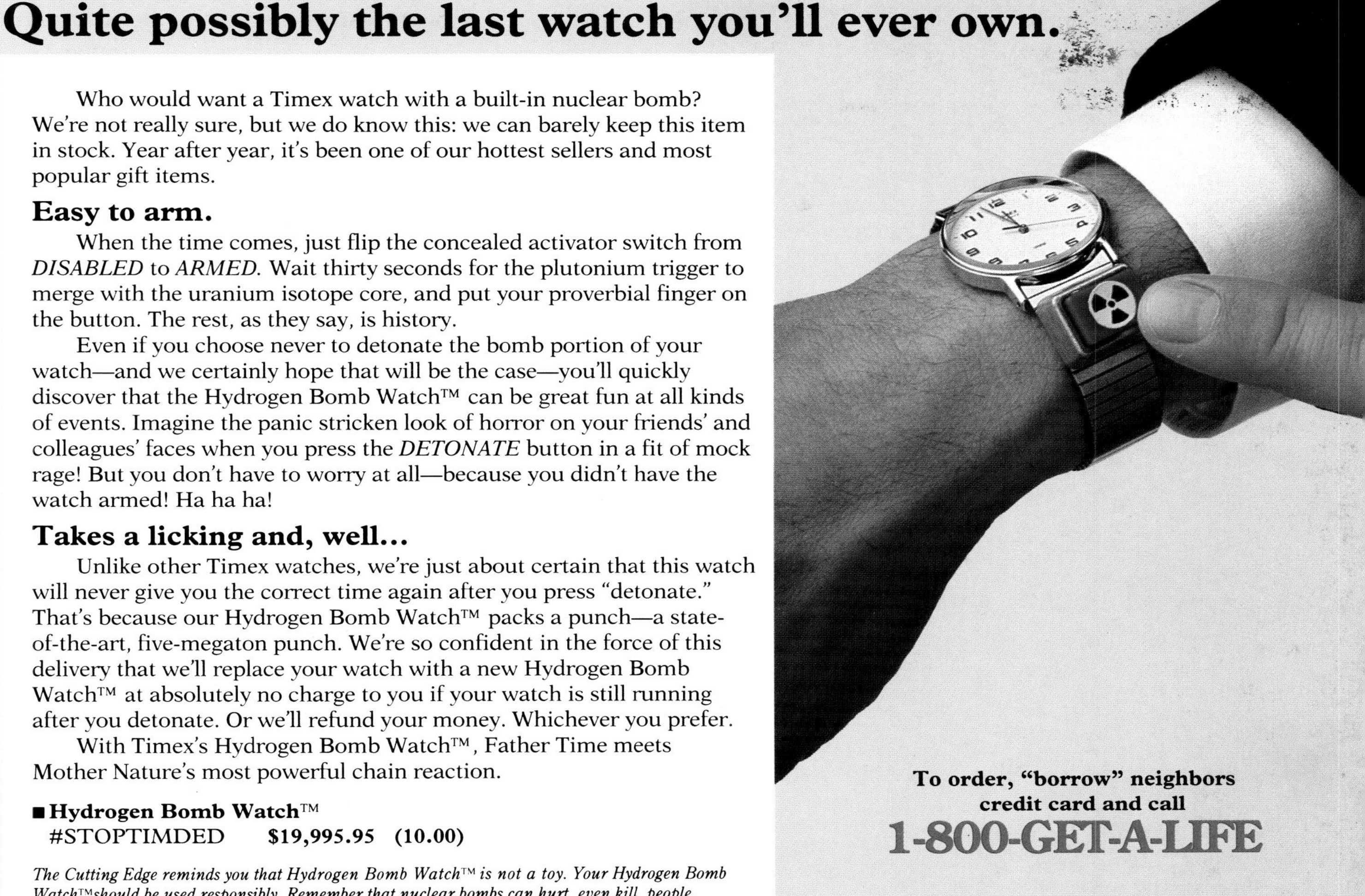

Who would want a Timex watch with a built-in nuclear bomb? We're not really sure, but we do know this: we can barely keep this item in stock. Year after year, it's been one of our hottest sellers and most popular gift items.

Easy to arm.

When the time comes, just flip the concealed activator switch from *DISABLED* to *ARMED.* Wait thirty seconds for the plutonium trigger to merge with the uranium isotope core, and put your proverbial finger on the button. The rest, as they say, is history.

Even if you choose never to detonate the bomb portion of your watch—and we certainly hope that will be the case—you'll quickly discover that the Hydrogen Bomb Watch™ can be great fun at all kinds of events. Imagine the panic stricken look of horror on your friends' and colleagues' faces when you press the *DETONATE* button in a fit of mock rage! But you don't have to worry at all—because you didn't have the watch armed! Ha ha ha!

Takes a licking and, well...

Unlike other Timex watches, we're just about certain that this watch will never give you the correct time again after you press "detonate." That's because our Hydrogen Bomb Watch™ packs a punch—a state-of-the-art, five-megaton punch. We're so confident in the force of this delivery that we'll replace your watch with a new Hydrogen Bomb Watch™ at absolutely no charge to you if your watch is still running after you detonate. Or we'll refund your money. Whichever you prefer.

With Timex's Hydrogen Bomb Watch™, Father Time meets Mother Nature's most powerful chain reaction.

■ **Hydrogen Bomb Watch™**
#STOPTIMDED **$19,995.95 (10.00)**

The Cutting Edge reminds you that Hydrogen Bomb Watch™ is not a toy. Your Hydrogen Bomb Watch™ should be used responsibly. Remember that nuclear bombs can hurt, even kill, people. All purchasers must include valid Department of Defense nuclear materials purchase certificate. Convicted felons must wait seven days before purchase. Please do not take your Hydrogen Bomb Watch™ to conventional jewelers for repairs—always return to an NRC-authorized service center.

A secretary on wheels.

Press the *activate protocol* button on AutoStaple™ and say "good-bye" to your desk full of cluttered papers.

AutoStaple™ is the world's only *mobile* document scanner. Combining a precision guidance system originally intended for the Patriot Missile and a deft mobility derived from the MX mobile launcher array program, AutoStaple™ brings state-of-the-art defense research into your office.

This multipurpose stapler drives itself around your office, stopping at the closest unstapled papers to sort by topic, collate, and staple together similar documents. Documents are sorted neatly by page number, stapled, and left stacked—just where they were found. And with its "search and destroy" feature, you can enter up to 150 subject headings on the pop-up LCD screen and your stapler will then locate any and all documents containing any one of these subjects in its text. Once located, these documents will then be promptly shredded with AutoStaple™'s solar-powered onboard shredder.

Order AutoStaple™ today, and you can fire your secretary tomorrow.

■ **AutoStaple™ with Search and Destroy**
#MXSTPLE **$6,999.95 (3.50)**

Sorry, AutoStaple™ cannot be sold outside of the US, nor to foreign nationals.

Now you can pump your *very own* gas.

Never wait again in a gas line at some tacky convenience store with your own Off Shore Oil Rig. With the purchase of an oil well, worries about the international oil supply, foreign wars, and trade embargoes are gone forever.

The Cutting Edge has purchased these oil rigs from well-known multinational oil corporations, who find that these particular wells do not produce enough oil to be profitable. For the average family, however, these wells will produce more than enough oil to keep the tank topped off on the auto and the powerboat for years to come.

Each well comes complete with all necessary equipment, including derricks, primary and secondary pump stations, platforms, and 5,000 feet of seven-inch steel casings. (Work crews not included.) A 35-page instruction manual guides you through all facets of the operation of your Off Shore Oil Rig. Refinery not included.

■ **Off Shore Oil Rig** #ECODISASTR **$175,000.00**
EPA permits may be required for operation.

Free gift-wrap!

To order, call standing on your head
1-800-NO-WAY

MAKE A STATEMENT

Own your own bank. At these prices you may want two!

Through a unique, specially negotiated agreement with the Federal Deposit Insurance Corporation, The Cutting Edge has acquired a large number of banks. Many of these banks are well-known, "high-profile" businesses, some of which were highly successful during the "go-go" years of the 1980s. All banks are sold "as is," but are 100% complete, with main office, at least three branches, a full complement of staff, and at least 100 depositors. Each bank also comes with "no-fault" FDIC deposit insurance. And many banks even include up to 100 ATM locations!

Your own executive offices.

Even if you only drop by once a month, we guarantee that you will have your own executive office suite, and that everyone in the bank will know your name and greet you respectfully.

Is there a more conclusive sign that you've arrived other than owning your own bank? We don't think so.

■ **Your Very Own Bank**
#MYOWNBNK **$200,000.00**

A Planet of Your Very Own.

Ever since the Dutch bought Manhattan from the Indians for a handful of wampum, the acquisition of large tracts of real estate at a bargain price has been a certain sign of business acumen. These days, though, it's practically impossible to find that truly special parcel of land here on earth. That's why you should consider looking to the skies—with Century 22.

A name you can trust. Century 22.

Working alongside astronomers from NASA's Jet Propulsion Lab, Century 22 agents have scoured the Milky Way galaxy searching for suitable planets. Many planets that they found were too close to their suns and had rather warm surfaces. Others were too far away, and were completely encased in sheets of ice several miles thick. Still others appeared to be on the verge of being sucked into nearby black holes. All of these planets were rejected. Only the crème de la crème were selected and are now listed for sale by Century 22.

Location. Location. Location!

Because all of our planets are carefully screened, we can assure you that your planet will support all higher life forms, including most vertebrates. You are guaranteed that there will be at least 20% oxygen in the atmosphere, plenty of water (note: water may need to be melted), and surface temperatures will not range above 150° nor below –100° Fahrenheit. Best of all, if you're not completely satisfied with your planet when you arrive, Century 22 will exchange your planet for a new planet free of charge!

Next-door neighbors are 10,000 light-years away.

Close your eyes and imagine windswept and glacier covered mountain ranges towering to 50,000 feet. And canyons hundreds of times deeper and longer than Earth's Grand Canyon. Imagine all this—and your nearest neighbors are more than 10,000 light-years away...

Worried about uninvited visitors? For an extra $1,500.00, we'll send a continuous intergalactic digital message, alerting others that your planet is private property and trespassing is strictly prohibited.

All planets come complete with title, clear and free, and a deeded easement. Here is a unique real estate investment opportunity with long-term—real long-term—growth potential.

- **A Planet of Your Very Own** #LTSOFPOTNTIAL **$125,000.00**
- **"No Trespassing" Radio Message (100 years continuous transmission)** #DNTEVNTHNKOFLNDNGHERE! **$1,500.00**

Potential purchasers should realize that transportation is presently not technologically feasible.

Not approved by the FDA

Now you can get two, three times the work done with CloneMate™!

If you're like a lot of busy people, you've probably thought before about how much additional work you could accomplish in a day if only you could clone yourself.

Only a few years ago, cloning was a field best left to science fiction enthusiasts. Today, however, thanks to several bold innovations in biotech research, cloning has become a reality.

Let us make you a new person.

After a thorough pre-cloning physical and psychological profile examination, you will be admitted to the CloneMate™ laboratory and positioned inside the CloneMate™ receptor unit. Here, deep inside a device similar to a CAT scanner, each and every molecule in your body will be replicated in the adjacent clone incubator cylinder. And don't worry—with our new cloning process, everything will be faithfully copied—from the stored chemical memories in your brain, right on down to the dirt underneath your fingernails.

Send in the clones.

Imagine—now you can work simultaneously in three cities. Or, have your clone work while you vacation. Feeling uninspired at work? Try *calling yourself up* to bounce ideas off *yourself*. Looking for a second opinion? Ask your clone! Sick and tired of working Mondays? Send in your clone. The possibilities are endless.

- **CloneMate™ - First Clone**
  #COPYME **$195,000.00**
- **Each Additional Clone**
  #1MORTIMWNTKILME
  $65,000.00

Warning: One percent of all users of CloneMate™ will experience a complete and irreversible psychotic break during the cloning process. If you happen to find yourself in this one percent, please accept our apologies along with a gift certificate for $100.00.

Extra brain tackles tough jobs.

Using our new Xtra Brain™ is a real "no-brainer." Simply attach the color-coded electrodes to the left and right hemispheres of the cerebral cortex on your Xtra Brain™. Next, place the other end of each electrode cable on your skull, following the handy schematic diagram. Now take a few deep breaths, close your eyes, and gently place your Xtra Brain™ into the supplied electrically charged gel-filled Brain Jar™. Like magic, Xtra Brain™ will come to life instantaneously. And before you know it, you'll be hard at work with more energy, ideas, and sheer thinking power than ever before!

Please order your Xtra Brain™ by the pound. Order *Geraldo* for small and relatively simple jobs, *Bob* for common tasks, and request the top of the line *Spock* model for complex or abstract thinking. All brains are packed in dry ice in FDA-approved live organ transport containers and shipped overnight via Federal Express.

■ **Geraldo** (Under 3 pounds)	#GERALDO	**$495.95**	**(5.00)**
■ **Bob** (3 to 5 pounds)	#BOB	**$995.95**	**(27.50)**
■ **Spock** (Over 5 pounds)	#SPOCK	**$1,325.95**	**(30.00)**

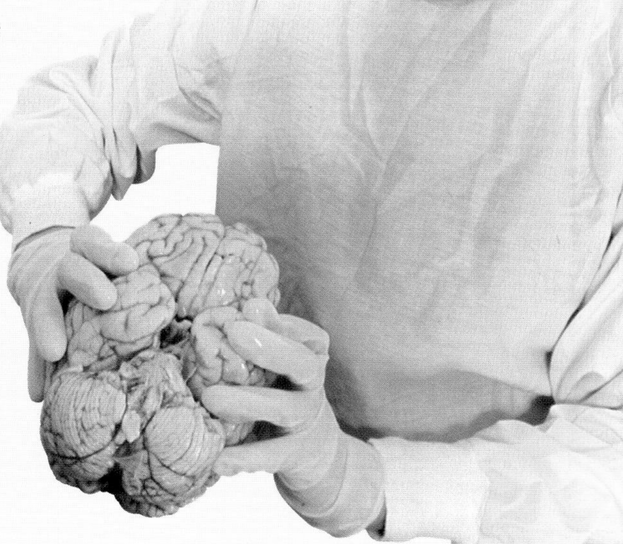

Small size Geraldo Xtra Brain™

THE FAST TRACK!

To order, ask your clone to call
1-800-LOOK-MA-NO-HANDS

Don't walk to work. Run.

The Cutting Edge Executive Sportswear line makes getting to work a workout.

Our exclusive design looks good, smells better.

When you first slip into your Executive Sportswear shirt and suit, you'll notice the generous cut. There's enough room here to jump high hurdles. Seams are triple sewn with 100-pound-test nylon fishing line. Patented Pore-tex™ fabric sucks up perspiration. Heat-activated fibers embedded deep within the Pore-tex™ fabric release fresh scents to mask abrasive perspiration odors. The more you work out, the better you smell.

You'll also find that our exclusive design fits your busy lifestyle. Light-reflective filaments in your necktie are woven into an attractive and functional design. As you run home from the office your necktie reflects oncoming car headlights. Here is a tie that can actually *save your life.*

Three different sizes. Three different smells.

The Executive Sportswear line is available in three sizes (S, M, and L) and three Pore-tex™ scents: *Men At Sea, Lilac Summer Eve,* or *Cherry Pop.* Never needs cleaning.

Men's Executive Sportswear
Shirt, Pants, Jacket & Tie

- **Grey Pin Stripe** #MRSWET5K **$895.95 (15.00)**
- **Navy Blue** #MRSWET10K **$895.95 (15.00)**

Woman's Executive Sportswear
Blouse, Skirt, Jacket & Ascot

- **Grey Pin Stripe** #MSSWET5K **$995.95 (15.00)**
- **Navy Blue** #MSSWET10K **$995.95 (15.00)**

Please indicate size and scent when ordering.

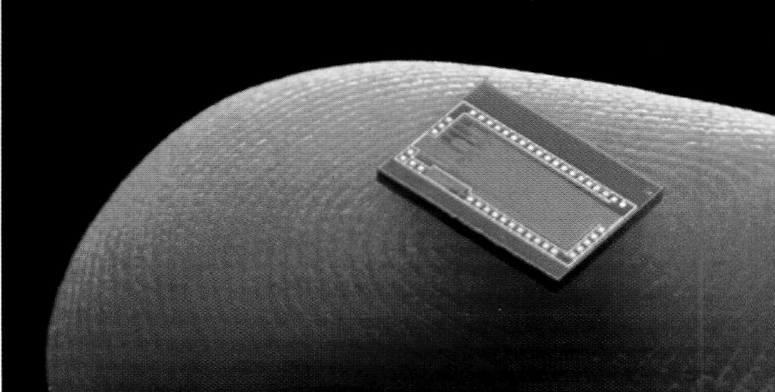

Sweet Dreams™ child-implanted microprocessor

Office On The Go.™
For the go-go executive.

Office On The Go™ is about staying in touch. Really in touch. Like seven voice lines and three long distance carriers. Three fax lines. Two data lines, including one 24,000 Baud modem and one T1 digital data stream transmission network. Add the optional flip-down Visoscreen™, and Office On The Go™ adds video-conferencing capability!

None of this would be possible without RCA's Satcom 1, one of the world's most advanced telecommunications satellites. Stationed in a geosynchronous Earth orbit, Satcom 1 receives all the data from your Office On The Go™ telecommunications headgear, simultaneously retransmitting it to one of ten giant Earth downlink facilities. And that means complete, uninterrupted telecommunications, wherever you are. From Madison Avenue to Mongolia, South Boston to the South Pole. *You're in touch.*

It's expandable. Real expandable.

If all that capability still doesn't sound like enough for you, be sure to order the optional Fiber Optic Cable. Simply hook the cable into the nearest telephone pole, and you'll have the telecommunications facilities of a small city surrounding your head—including your own area code and long distance routing capabilities.

Use your head and get ahead, with Office On The Go™.

- **Office On The Go™** #TLKINGHD **$1,955.95 (35.00)**
- **Visoscreen™** #HIMOM **$495.95 (15.00)**
- **Fiber Optic Cable** #POLEHKUP **$49.95 (10.00)**

Exclusively mail order!

To order, dial "O" and ask phone operator to call

1-800-YOUR-MOTHER-WEARS-ARMY-BOOTS

THE FASTER TRACK!

Child "on," child "off."

Time for baby Samantha to take a nap? Is Trevor a bit too wild today? Reach out for some high-tech help with Sweet Dreams™ from Totlogic, Inc.

Simply grab for the Sweet Dreams™ remote controller and select from one of ten standard modes, including *VOLUME DOWN, MUTE* and *CHANGE CHANNELS* (to *SLEEP* or *HAPPY TIME*). Simply point and press, and the child-implanted microprocessor goes right to work, turning your command into reality. It's as easy to use as your TV remote control. In fact, if you misplace your Sweet Dreams™ remote control, you can use your TV control. It works just as well!

The story of the youthful cerebral cortex and a 32-bit "on board" computer.

Sweet Dreams™ is a product that is truly the meeting of two worlds—a growing brain stem and the latest in high-tech microcomputer wizardry. Totlogic, Inc., the innovative manufacturer of Sweet Dreams™, places a microcomputer deep in your child's brain in an unused portion of the cerebral cortex. It is here, in the "master control" of your child's brain, where Totlogic gently but efficiently alters electrical activity. Working in conjunction with a small series of computerized relays implanted in the thalamus, Sweet Dreams™ stops sensory impulses before they have a chance to get routed to the "higher centers" of the brain. But all you see is a small infrared detector that protrudes less than one one-hundredth of an inch above your child's scalp. It is practically undetectable. And best of all, the all-but-painless procedure required to install this high-tech gadgetry can be performed on an outpatient basis. It's really no more complicated than having a hang nail removed.

Order today, and we'll throw in the minor outpatient pediatric brain surgery for free. Includes 60-day warranty.

■ **Sweet Dreams**™ #GO2SLEP **$1,745.00 (3.00)**

Peva™ A name you can trust for multipurpose handwear.

Ever wish there was a truly multipurpose piece of handwear? One that would be just as much at home grilling a steak as it was fielding foul balls at a White Sox game? Well, finally you can put away all those miscellaneous pairs of special-purpose mitts and gloves, and slip on a pair of Pevas™, the finest multipurpose glove available anywhere.

Pevas™ are constructed of a durable automotive-type rubber manufactured by France's Michelin Corporation. With Michelin's quality rubber, your Pevas™ will handle years of abuse and they'll always look and feel great. Comfortable Velcro straps assure a snug fit, while hundreds of raised microdots on Pevas™' inner lining stimulate and energize tired palms and fingers. Best of all, you'll be pleasantly surprised by the wide range of temperatures at which Pevas™ feel comfortable. Even changing a flat tire in a twenty below blizzard is a "can-do" proposition for Pevas™!

Whether you're weeding the garden, playing a serious game of handball, or just typing a memo at the office, you'll soon discover what Peva™ fans have known all along: one hand in a Peva™ is worth two in the raw. Peva Gloves™. They're always up to the task at hand.

■ **Peva Gloves™** #ALLTHMBS **$49.95 (5.00)**

It's so real you'll think you're walking up stairs.

A three-minute workout on Prefab's Stairs™ provides the most complete form of body conditioning, aside from major reconstructive cosmetic surgery, that is currently available. Prefab™ is a leader in easy-to-assemble home exercise equipment, and Stairs™ is the most technologically advanced climber you can buy. One workout a month is all it takes for profound and irreversible aerobic, anaerobic, and anabolic changes in conditioning.

Up and down. Up and down.

With each step up Stairs™ you climb higher, higher, and higher. First you work out all of the major muscle groups in your right leg and foot as you move your right foot up onto the first stair. The patented non-slip surface insures firm footing. Now extend your workout to your left side. Move your left foot up onto the first step next to your right foot. Shock absorbing particle board cushions each and every step, eliminating costly bone spur surgery associated with other forms of exercising and body conditioning.

Increase your cardiovascular workout by taking a full range step. Move one foot up alongside the other foot and continue your forward motion as you drive your foot up to a yet higher step. At step three, your workout continues with the exclusive *WALK-DOWN*™ feature that sets this climber apart from all others. Now you are walking *down,* step by step, *backwards* as you "recondition" the same muscle groups that you conditioned on your way up.

Now you are down and it's time to go up again. Up and down. Up and down. Up and down. That's the key to Prefab's Stairs™.

Feels like the real thing.

Many people report that a workout on Stairs™ is the closest thing they've ever experienced to climbing up and down *actual* stairs.

Order Stairs™ today and discover for yourself what body conditioning is all about.

- **Prefab Stairs™ 3STEP**
  #NOSWET123 **$399.95 (65.00)**
- **Prefab Stairs™ 5STEP**
  #NOSWET12345 **$499.95 (95.00)**

Sorry,  *delivery not available.*

Wienie Steamer Slide Viewer.™

What is it about watching a slide show that always puts you in the mood for a perfectly steamed frank?

With our new Wienie Steamer Slide Viewer™, you get the best of Kodak projection and Waring frank steamers. The slide projection portion of the tabletop unit features high-quality Japanese optics, a bright halogen bulb, and a wide-screen viewing surface. Look around back, and you'll be pleasantly surprised to find a commercial-grade frankfurter steamer compartment. Don't let the small compartment size fool you—our Wienie Steamer Slide Viewer™ can steam up to six franks simultaneously—more than enough capacity for the whole party!

Family and friends will enjoy your vacation slides more than ever, knowing that great tasting franks are part of the show!

■ **Wienie Steamer Slide Viewer™** #UNEEDONEFRSURE **$95.95 (10.00)**

Smart Suck™ from Sashimi. This sucker is smart!

If you've ever wondered whether something you've been looking for has been sucked up into your vacuum cleaner, now you can know for sure. Sashimi's Smart Suck™ vacuum cleaner prints a detailed report of *everything* it has sucked up.

Sashimi's Smart Suck™ uses a proprietary ultrasound interpretive circuit to quickly and accurately identify up to 100,000 items commonly found while vacuuming—everything from Saint Bernard dog hair to Ecuador's "sucre" currency! It even identifies 100 different insects and 30 types of household dust! When Smart Suck™'s vacuum bag is filled, a complete printout is generated and plasticized for easy attachment to the bag. Looking for a missing item? Just check the printouts on your filled bags.

Now you can vacuum away and never worry again about what's being sucked up into the bag. Because with Smart Suck™—nothing is gone for good!

■ **Smart Suck Vacuum™**
#NRDVACUM **$695.95 (25.00)**

Smart Suck™'s detailed report answers the question: "What's in the bag?"

100,000 evergreens in your bathroom.

Have you ever noticed that sometimes your bathroom just doesn't seem to have quite enough air? Perhaps you've tried traditional air fresheners, but to no avail. The reason? The problem is more than just odors. The problem is significantly lower air pressure in your bathroom. The solution? 100,000 Evergreens™ from Sashimi.

Oxygen's version of Nutrasweet.

100,000 Evergreens™ releases a unique oxygen substitute which looks and acts very much like regular oxygen, and even features many of the same benefits. When inhaled, the oxygen substitute perfuses through your pulmonary capillaries and bonds to your blood's hemoglobin just like old-fashioned oxygen. This oxygen substitute collects harmlessly in the tiny mitochondria, the "powerhouse" in each of your body's cells. Studies show that this oxygen substitute is ultimately deposited back into your bloodstream and safely released when you exhale.

While regular oxygen doesn't really smell like much of anything, our new oxygen-like substitute has been designed with a pleasant aroma equivalent to more than 100,000 evergreens. How much aroma power is that? Put it this way: if our product were a traditional air freshener, it would take up three city blocks!

Bring your bathroom to life with Sashimi's 100,000 Evergreens™.

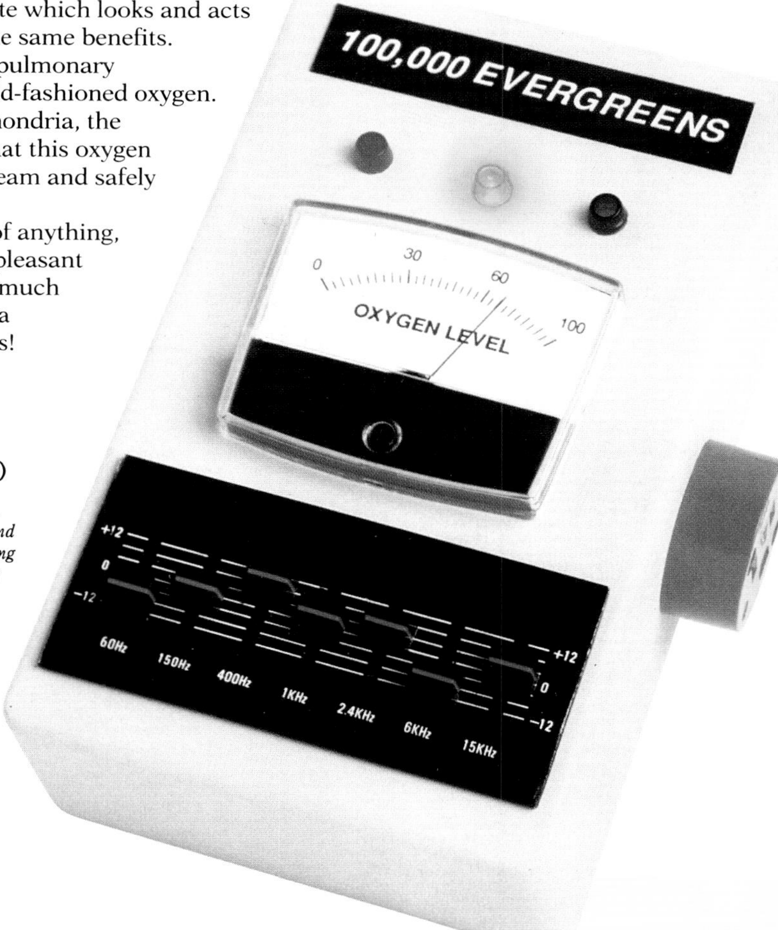

- **100,000 Evergreens™**
  #WNTEVRWRK $199.95 (7.50)

100,000 Evergreens™ is intended to complement, not replace, the oxygen in your bathroom. Always stay alert for the signs and symptoms of inadequate oxygen perfusion to the brain, including dizziness, numbness and tingling, and slurred speech. To treat for overuse of 100,000 Evergreens™, place victim in a hyperbaric chamber and pressurize to six atmospheres with pure oxygen.

Matzo Maker™ from Chutzpa Home Electric.

Making matzo with Matzo Maker™ is so easy even a gentile can do it. First, mix together wheat flour, egg yolks, salt, and water in the handy yarmulke-shaped measuring cup & stirring bowl. Pour one yarmulke's worth of your matzo mixture into Matzo Maker™ and adjust the cook selector for light matzo *(You call that baked?)* to dark matzo *(Oy, burnt again!)*. Then wait for the indicator light to flash. Best of all, you don't even have to wait for it to rise, and there's no dealing with unreliable yeast. Fresh matzo is ready in minutes.

Swiss Chocolate Matzo? You bet.

Along with every Matzo Maker™, you'll receive a special hardcover copy of Dr. Abraham Levinstein's Ph.D. thesis, ***Matzo: Fact and Fiction.*** Included are unique and exciting cross-cultural recipes like Guacamole Matzo, Pork Rind Matzo, Swiss Chocolate Matzo, and others. The true matzo lover in your family will also enjoy reading the fascinating 350-page section entitled, "The History of Matzo Through the Ages."

Each and every component used to make your Matzo Maker™ is blessed by Dr. Levinstein before it is assembled into the final product and shipped to you.

- **Matzo Maker™**
  #OYYUYOY $49.95 (6.50)

Own a piece of the rock. And reduce the Federal deficit at the same time!

Visible for miles around, the enormous busts of Abe Lincoln, Teddy Roosevelt, Thomas Jefferson, and George Washington have stood watch over the plains of South Dakota for more than five decades. Now, in an unprecedented effort to lower the Federal budget deficit, this one-of-a-kind treasure is being broken down into six-inch cubes and sold in bulk.

Each Rushmore Cube comes wrapped in a chamois cloth and is packaged in an attractive gift box. A handsome certificate documents from which president your cube came. We've even included a chart showing the original facial location of your cube.

Help put the good ol' U.S. of A. back in the black, as we dismantle an old and cherished symbol of our former greatness. Your Rushmore Cube is sure to become a family heirloom for generations to come. Order today.

- **Rushmore Cube** (Specify President)
  #ROCK **$24.95 (25.00)**

Please note that airfare, room, board, and $500 per diem per parent will be billed separately to your account. If you have ordered your Mom and Dad™ for life, and if either your new Mom or new Dad dies before you do, The Cutting Edge will provide a replacement Mom and Dad™ of our own selection at no additional charge to you.

MADE IN THE USA!!

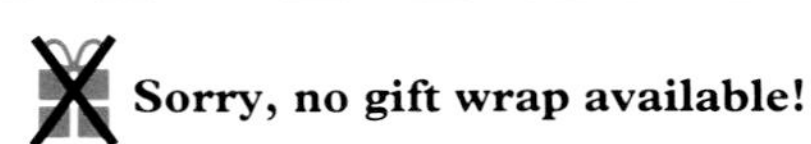

Sorry, no gift wrap available!

Mom and Dad.™ The way they were supposed to be.

If you've ever wished you could have someone else as your mother and father, well wish no more. The Cutting Edge is proud to offer, in time for the holidays, Mom and Dad™.

A match made in heaven. Sort of.

When you place your order, send us a photo of yourself, along with a brief physical description, and we will carefully select your new Mom and Dad™. With over 15,000 high quality moms and dads of all races and nationalities on file, your new Mom and Dad™ will be just what you're looking for. Whether you're a husky Southern redhead or a slender French blonde, our match will be so perfect that no one will know your secret. No one, that is, but you and Mom and Dad™. And that's the way it should be. Think of it as yet another one of the many hundreds of special little secrets that you'll share with your new parents.

Once you enter an order for your new Mom and Dad™, a Cutting Edge parental coordinator will conduct an exhaustive interview with you over the phone. Extraordinarily detailed information about you will then be committed to memory by your new parents. (In many cases, we find that your new Mom and Dad™ remember your childhood and other personal facts *better* than your actual, biological parents!)

"Mom, Dad.... I'd like you to meet Sarah."

Unlike many other parents, when your new Mom and Dad™ make their first appearance, you can trust them 100%! No embarrassing comments about your past behavior, no bizarre personality traits that need explanation or apologies—just charming, thoughtful discussion coupled with excellent manners, a well-groomed look, and tasteful and appropriate dress.

Every Mom and Dad™ comes with a clean bill of health, and are intelligent, hard-working individuals.

With Mom and Dad™, The Cutting Edge brings perfection to an imperfect world.

- **Mom and Dad™: One Event** (24 Hour Limit)
  #NWFLKS4ADAY **$1,500.00**
- **Mom and Dad™: For Life**
  #NWFLKS4LIFE **$500,000.00**

The American Bald Eagle. Now you can own a piece of American history.

Imagine a live American Bald Eagle, swooping over your yard, its seven-foot wingspan outstretched, prowling for rodents. Friends and neighbors will be amazed, as this living symbol of the ol' red, white, and blue circles your house all day, only to return to its indoor nest at sunset.

A footnote in the recently signed US-Mexican Free Trade Agreement enables us to purchase up to fifty of these majestic flyers directly from the Mexican Office of Wildlife each month. Your Bald Eagle will be delivered in a large crate, complete with a ten-pound nest, a week's supply of miscellaneous live rodents, and a copy of Roger Tory Peterson's bestseller, ***The American Bald Eagle: The Killer from the Skies.***

Next July Fourth, don't just fly the ol' red, white, and blue. Fly something bigger. Show your true colors, with an American Bald Eagle.

- **American Bald Eagle**
  #ILLGLALEN **$199.95 (30.00)**

Wild bald eagles can be extremely dangerous, and may attack pets and small children without warning. Some eagles may carry diseases such as tuberculosis and rabies.

To order, eat apple pie, shoot a gun and call

1-800-RAH-RAH

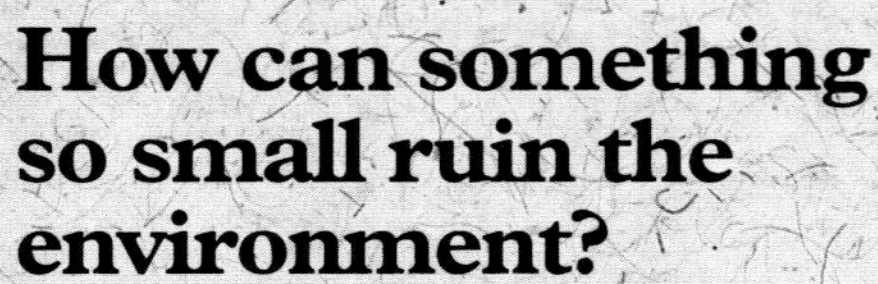

How can something so small ruin the environment?

That's what most people think when they think about *staples*. And that's precisely why staples have become such a serious threat to our environment. Because they're so small, no one bothers to recycle them! Yet, next to disposable diapers, staples are now filling up our landfills faster than anything.

To use the Green Staple Machine™, simply drop used or damaged staples into the top-mounted staple debris funnel. Next, set the casting mold to one of three sizes: *SMALL* (dime), *MEDIUM* (nickel), or *LARGE* (quarter). When the Green Staple Machine™ senses that enough staples are present, the diecast mold will automatically cast another staple slug, using the same high-impact cold-molding technology that the federal government uses to make currency.

Order Green Staple Machine™ today. Because if we don't act soon, the earth will be stapled to death.

■ **Green Staple Machine**™
#NVRPAYFRPRKNGAGAIN! **$49.95 (8.00)**

To order, call while levitating
1-800-UMMMMMMMMM

Now smokers can do their part to save the earth!

If you're a smoker, being Earth friendly hasn't been easy. Exhaled, "secondary smoke" goes right up into the stratosphere, where it interacts with sunlight to create dangerous carbon dioxide, worsening the greenhouse effect. But now, with Marlboro's Smoker's Helmet™, you can smoke away guilt free.

Smoker's Helmet™ is a 100% "closed-circuit" breathing apparatus—similar, in fact, to a traditional scuba tank. This means that no air can enter or exit the helmet—everything is recycled, over and over and over again. When you exhale, smoke is sucked into the rear-mounted vacuum unit, where a carbon filter removes large nicotine particles. This pre-filtered, used air is then routed through the transporter hose to the neck filtration unit. It is here that your used air is forced through a series of chemically treated osmotic filters, which react with the dirty air to create ample quantities of relatively clean air. A three-ounce waste receptacle unit collects filtered smoke waste and used filtration chemicals. (Replace unit every three months or 100 packs, whichever comes first.)

EPA approved and endorsed by the Tobacco Institute. Can be used with pipes and cigars under eight inches in length.

■ **Smoker's Helmet**™
#CNCERHED **$295.95 (17.50)**

BUY SOMETHING TODAY. ANYTHING.

Generate surplus oxygen in EcoDome™'s unique rain forest microclimate.

After years of breathing her clean, fresh air, isn't it time you gave a little "0_2" back to Mother Earth? With EcoDome™ you're part of the solution—not the problem.

EcoDome™ works its oxygen magic thanks to three super-dense photosynthetic flora zones—just like a larger, conventional rain forest. From ground level grasses, on through to the mid-vegetation zone, and, ultimately, the dense forest canopy, the chlorophyll in EcoDome™'s array of photosynthetic plants are continually converting sunlight into oxygen. It's a process that's been going on for millions and millions of years, and now you can watch it happen in the privacy of your own home.

EcoDome™'s biosphere comes encased in a photo-transparent Lexan dome. A tiny one-way valve at the top of the dome permits oxygen to exit—your perpetual gift to Mother Nature—a way of saying, "*thanks for everything*."

Over the course of its natural life, your EcoDome™ will produce about a quarter of a million atoms of oxygen—enough to support a small house pet for eight to ten minutes.

Thank Mother Nature for all those years of support, with EcoDome™.

■ **EcoDome**™ #THS0_2ISONME **$69.95 (5.00)**

Simulated recycled paper.

LampMan.™

Did you know that lights left on around the house and office account for more than 30% of the wasted electricity in the United States? If turning lights on and off is too much for you, here's a bright idea— LampMan™.

The first thing you'll notice about LampMan™ is the stylish, modern design—part Bauhaus, part Le Corbusier. Look underneath and you'll notice the ultra-comfortable truss and the padded plush cotton harness. You'll find that LampMan™ is as comfortable to wear after 18 hours of continuous use as it was the moment you got out of bed and strapped it on.

Strap it on and go!

Using LampMan™ is a snap. First thing in the morning, back up to LampMan™ and align your lumbar vertebrae with the silk-screened symbols on the harness. Tighten the Velcro truss, plug in the 400-foot retractable power cord, flip the light switch on, and you're on your way—with plenty of light for the whole day.

See the light. Order LampMan™ today and save the earth tomorrow.

■ **LampMan**™ #ICTHELGT **$99.95 (12.50)**

Harness the awesome power of the wind with Wind Beanie.™

Do your part to harness renewable energy sources, with our wind-powered, cranial-based Wind Beanie™ power generator system from Brooklyn's Yarmulke Electric.

Wind Beanie™ is constructed of durable stainless steel tubing and features permanently sealed and lubricated bearings and gear systems. The lightweight, brushless generator is installed in a weatherproof location, on the underside of the beanie, assuring years of trouble-free operation. As a thoughtful finishing touch, a handsome plaid design is imprinted on the beanie exterior. Before it came to market, Wind Beanie™ was tested high atop New Hampshire's Mount Washington, home of the "World's Worst Weather." There, amid eighty and ninety mph winds, scientists generated power surges equal to more than 50 kilowatts of alternating current. But you don't need a hurricane-force gust to get power from your beanie. Simply walking at a brisk six mile per hour pace for 12 hours will generate enough electricity to recharge four AA nicad batteries. And that's enough power to run your Walkman for almost forty-five minutes!

■ **Wind Beanie**™
#ELCTRPWERPLNTHED **$49.95 (5.00)**

Never use Wind Beanie™ during electrical storms.

Simulated recycled paper.

Home Recycling Center.™

Developed by some of the top interior designers and waste management experts in the country, our Home Recycling Center™ installs conveniently under many kitchen counters. Using the 100-page step-by-step installation manual, Home Recycling Center™ can be installed by three plumbers and an electrician in less than one week. (Please note that Home Recycling Center™ requires separate, three-phase AC line installed by your local utility.) And when your EPA-approved 100-foot smoke-stack is completed by a certified mason, you'll be all set to recycle away!

Lots of pressure. Lots of heat.

Once you select the type of input material, insert your waste and press *Activate Recycle Sequence.* The Home Recycling Center™ then gets down to business. First, home waste is sanitized in stage one, where steaming hot jets of sulfuric acid blast every square inch of waste. In stage two, waste is pulverized repeatedly with a 10,000 psi pneumatic titanium sledge. Once 500 pounds of recyclable waste is accrued, it enters stage three and drops down into our "Regeneration Pit™," the heart of the Home Recycling Center™. Here, a recessed, lead-lined oven melts home waste in seconds, using temperatures of over 2,000° centigrade. Finally, in stage four the newly recycled product is poured into a gigantic cast iron mold. After six hours of forced air cooling, the freshly recycled material is automatically conveyored out of the system to you!

Three exciting molds.

When you order your Home Recycling Center™ you can chose from three exciting heavy duty cast iron molds: *Juvenile Lawn Furniture* (produces a 26" high picnic table), *Studded Snow Tires* (produces size 185-13R only), or *Standard Bath Mat* (textured fish motif). Featuring a one and one-half ton design, quality control will never be a problem with these cast iron molds. We guarantee that your first picnic table (or studded snow tire or bath mat) will be of the exact same quality as number 100, or we will refund the purchase price of the lead mold.

Saving the planet starts at home, and what better way to show your commitment than with the purchase of your very own Home Recycling Center™? EPA permit required.

■ **Home Recycling Center™**
#WOW! **$28,500.00 (850.00)**

(Please specify mold choice: Juvenile Lawn Furniture, Studded Snow Tires, or Standard Bath Mat.)

Please note that Home Recycling Center™ will consume approximately 55,000 watts during operation. Surge suppressors are recommended.

SpudMaster™ — Your personal trainer.

If you've ever trained professionally, you know how helpful it can be to have a personal trainer take you through your workout. There is something about that personal contact providing encouragement, reward, and punishment when necessary, that is hard to put a price on. Until recently. Now we can put a price on it; an exact price in fact. Enter SpudMaster™—your personal trainer.

A real pro.

Unlike other personal trainers, you never have to wait for SpudMaster™. When you want to exercise, he's ready. Day or night. Here's a real pro who will custom design an aerobic or anaerobic workout to fit your needs. Or choose from one of over 100 pre-programmed workouts. From Jane Fonda to Richard Simmons, Step Reebok to U.S. Army Special Forces Tactical Training, SpudMaster™ knows them all.

Sounds like Buddy Hackett.

Voice synthesis microchips give SpudMaster™ his voice. In a voice strikingly reminiscent of Buddy Hackett, your personal trainer will take you step by step through your exercise regimen. First, he'll explain how to perform the exercise. Then he'll count you through it, giving you lively encouragement when needed: *"Comm'on fatso, let's pick up the pace!"* SpudMaster™ will even break up the tedium of your daily routine with off-color jokes. Before long you'll learn not to laugh in the middle of bench pressing 200 pounds when you hear a familiar opening line such as *"Hey did ya hear the one 'bout the transvestite body builder...?"*

The big blue nose.

After your workout, hinge open SpudMaster™'s large blue nose to store your Evian, towels, and all your gym gear. A virtual locker room of space is to be found in your personal trainer's nasal cavity. Then sit back and relax as you pick up the latest in nutritional guidance from SpudMaster™'s exhaustive information data bank. SpudMaster™ even has helpful hints for you on how to diet when you're pregnant, how to come up "clean" for steroid testing, and a whole lot more.

Built from steel-reinforced fiberglass, SpudMaster™ is fire retardant, water-resistant to 250 feet, and can withstand 15 Gs of force. Here is a personal trainer that can go the distance and take you with him, whether you like it or not!

■ **SpudMaster™** #JSTDOIT! **$1,499.95 (120.00)**

To order, soak phone in gas, light match and quickly call

1-800-YABBA-DABBA-DO

"Now you know my secret."
–Oprah Winfrey
"SpudMaster™ is the personal trainer's trainer. I'm going to live to be 150 and SpudMaster™ is the reason why!"
–Jack La Lanne
SpudMaster™ is not only your personal trainer— he's also your best friend!
delivery not recommended.

Finally. Legal advice you can afford from Pocket Lawyer.™

"Your honor, my client pleads not guilty."

Not too long ago, we were being sued a lot. A whole lot. People were saying that some of our products didn't live up to our claims; something about "false advertising." We were desperate. Real desperate. That's when we spotted an ad in the classified section of **The Wall Street Journal.** So we gave it a shot. The results were astounding.

The verdict is in—you win!

After we got Pocket Lawyer™, we started winning cases. Left and right. And something else started to happen. We stopped getting sued. Everyone knew that we had the best legal advice in town that money could buy.

More than just a computer brain.

As testimony begins, press the *EVIDENCE IN* button. Pocket Lawyer™ listens intently to every word, cross-referencing every word and phrase with over 30,000 programmed precedents, rulings, and cases, from lower circuit courts all the way up to the U.S. Supreme Court. You'll be amazed as Pocket Lawyer™ interjects motions, pleadings, and objections, right as the trial or hearing is taking place.

But Pocket Lawyer™ is more than just the world's most powerful legal brain. It can also think, interpret, and, when necessary, *act decisively on its own.* Plus, you get to decide which legal approach is right for you: *L.A. LAW, CLARENCE THOMAS, F. LEE BAILEY* or *DERSHOWITZ.*

Tested in the heat of battle.

Guess who really won the William Kennedy Smith rape trial. Now guess again. That's right! Through it all, a team of Pocket Lawyers™ worked day and night, building a case so solid not even the best prosecutors could find an opening.

Get Pocket Lawyer™ today. Before your competitor does.

- **Pocket Lawyer™ - American Legal Code**
  #PLUSA **$995.95 (4.50)**
- **Pocket Lawyer™ - Islamic Laws**
  #PLIRAN **$995.95 (4.50)**
- **Pocket Lawyer™ - International Drug Law**
  #PLDOPE **$995.95 (4.50)**

REACH FOR SOME

Our toilet paper dispenser has a brain for TP.

Sleek Italian design and state-of-the-art microprocessor technology combine for a toilet paper dispenser that is out of this world.

As your hand approaches the roll, infrared detectors alert TPBrain™ to move from *STANDBY MODE* to *ACTIVE USE.* TPBrain™ Dispenser alerts you if remaining tissues fall below "MTR," that is, *minimum tissues required* for one visit to the WC. LCD screen reads "DON'T GO!" and an audible "distress alarm" sounds. (You preset TPBrain™'s distress alarm to sound when you want it to because only you know how many tissues is not enough.) As you roll off sheets, TPBrain™'s scanners keep track of the exact number of sheets dispensed. As you approach optimum number of sheets to use per visit—again preset by you—audible tones increase in frequency. When you reach "BUTT," or *best use of toilet tissue,* servo-controlled locks secure the dispenser roll in place. No additional tissues will be issued this visit. Finally, you can put an end to toilet paper wastage for good!

Installs in seconds for a lifetime of service. After just one use, you'll never accept paper from any other dispenser again.

TPBrain™ Dispenser #WHY? **$99.95 (5.50)**

Take a shower with Vanna. With Washman Microsoap™ TV.

Because Washman Microsoap™ TV features the same hydrophobic coating used on the hulls of ocean liners, Washman's LCD screen actually repels water, assuring you a crystal-clear picture in the shower. And Washman operates almost entirely at low voltages, so the risk of electrocution is minimal.

Your Washman TV comes complete with a detachable 30-foot, double-insulated AC cord and connections for VCR, cable, and external antenna. And when you've washed all the way down to the Washman television, simply insert Washman into a fresh bar of our specially configured Irish Spring hypoallergenic soap.

Next time you shower, don't miss your favorite soap on TV. Get Washman Microsoap™ TV .

- **Washman Microsoap™ TV**
  #SLPRYTV **$495.95 (5.00)**
- **Irish Spring Washman Soap (Box of 6)**
  #SOAP4TV **$30.95 (3.00)**

Free gift-wrap!

To order, call after a double shot of espresso

1-800-HOW-MUCH-WOOD-WOULD-A-WOODCHUCK-CHUCK-IF-A-WOODCHUCK-COULD-CHUCK-WOOD?

HIGH-TECH HELP

Meal Reporter™ tells you what you need to know. *Before* you eat it.

With Meal Reporter™, you know what you're going to eat *before* you eat it.

To use Meal Reporter™, simply insert the food probe into your entree at least one inch, stir vigorously, and wait two minutes. When the *ANALYSIS COMPLETE* alarm beeps, remove Meal Reporter™. To hear the results of the analysis, gently clean off the probe, place the very same end of the probe into your ear, and listen to the five-minute analysis of your meal presented in a pleasing feminine voice.

Meal Reporter™ not only gives you verification that you got what you ordered—it also provides a detailed nutrient analysis, complete pesticide residue report, and information on the presence of dangerous bacteria as well as pest and rodent droppings.

Eat, drink, and be merry—no matter what restaurant you're in. With Meal Reporter™.

- **Meal Reporter™**
  #IWDNTEATITIFIWERU
  $195.95 (3.50)

Roadmaster Navigational System.™ You're in good hands with R.N.S.™

Have you ever used a macro for your computer? Those simple little programs that repeat mindless routines with the press of a button? We've taken the macro concept out of the computer and placed it where it can do you the most good—right under the hood of your car.

Designed and tested by ace driver Jackie Stewart.

When we thought R.N.S.™ was ready to be released to the public, we turned to one of the best race car drivers in the world to help us test the prototype—Scottish driving star Jackie Stewart. And when Jackie tested Roadmaster™ Version 0.1, he went all out. Like 150 to 200 miles per hour on the Le Mans course. And 18 days on the trans-Sahara overland route. And 36 continuous hours at the Bonneville Salt Flats proving grounds in Utah. In three months, Jackie went through 17 prototypes and just as many vehicles. But it was worth it. We've been able to find and correct just about every bug in this revolutionary automotive steering system. R.N.S.™ is now ready for you. (By the way, Jackie's doing fine and says "thanks for the cards." He should be back on the road after a few months of physical therapy.)

Record, playback, and relax.

If you can operate a VCR, you can operate R.N.S.™ Set Roadmaster™ to *RECORD* and drive your most commonly travelled routes. Roadmaster™ records each and every turn and stop along the way. If you make a 73-degree left-hand turn at 33 mph 4.66 minutes into your commute, that's *exactly* the way Roadmaster™ will record and remember your turn. The next time you travel the recorded route, simply select the desired destination, press *GO*, and sit back and relax. All you have to do is start your car!

Turn the morning commute into the most relaxing moment of the day with Roadmaster Navigational System™.

- **Roadmaster Navigational System™**
  #LKMOMNOHNDS! **$1,485.00 (25.00)**

Warning: Roadmaster™ Version 1.1 may contain some software bugs, particularly in "Yield" and "School Crossing" subroutines. The Cutting Edge recommends that you always keep one eye on the road.

MR. MOTORHEAD

To order, clean grease from beneath your nails and call

1-800-AUTO-JUNK

Big tires. For people in a big hurry.

Never get stuck in aggravating rush hour traffic again, with new Cruncher Big Tires™ from Commuter Solutions, Inc. Annoying delays will be a thing of the past, as you shift into low gear and actually drive *over* congested traffic.

Cruncher Big Tires™ are made with eighteen separate steel belts, and feature a patented seven-inch deep megagrip tread pattern. Because each tire weighs nearly a full ton, you can drive in full confidence, knowing that you've got solid traction, whether you're driving over messy roadways covered with water, snow, or ice—or even if you're motoring over crushed steel and rubber.

Cruncher Big Tires™ can be installed in about four hours per tire, with standard pneumatic power wrenches and hydraulic winches.

- **Cruncher Big Tires**™ (1 Tire)
  #SPLAT **$890.00 (120.00)**

The Cutting Edge does not condone use of Cruncher Big Tires™ to drive over other vehicles. Such use may cause injury, even death, to other drivers. The Cutting Edge reminds you to drive defensively and to respect the rights of other motorists.

Must be shipped via *freight.*

A Close Shave At 70. From CarShave Caddy.™

If you've ever shaved on your way to work you know how tricky that can be. Keeping things "tied down," like your razor, shaving cream, and after-shave, can be a real hassle. Especially when you're going fast. Like 70 or 80. Who wants to fumble around for a styptic pencil at those kinds of speeds?

Another problem is cold shaving cream. If you want to go to work, and not to the emergency room, you'll want your razor to really glide over your face.

The solution? CarShave Caddy™ from Commuter Solutions, Inc.

A close shave at 70.

The first time we tested CarShave Caddy™, we were immediately impressed. What a rush. We almost hit a school bus. I guess our driver wasn't paying attention—after all, he was busy shaving. But let me tell you, that was some close shave!

The secret is hot crankcase oil.

CarShave Caddy™'s close shave comes from having hot cream right on board. A ¼ HP electric pump delivers a smooth supply of hot oil directly from the crankcase of your automobile through the patented *wrap-o-round*™ coils that surround your can of cream. (Safety valves insure against dangerous oil pressure buildup.) The oil circulates around the shaving cream can, and that's what makes the cream hot. Real hot.

Plus, there's a place to put everything you need. CarShave Caddy™'s precision molded receptacles hold your razor, blades, cream, and styptic pencil. It's all right in front of your face. You don't even need a mirror.

CarShave Caddy™ is guaranteed to last as long as your car does, or until your auto insurance is revoked. Whichever comes first.

Please note that CarShave Caddy™ requires the use of standard automotive welder's equipment for installation.

■ **CarShave Caddy™** #FSTSHAVE **$79.95 (12.50)**

CarShave Caddy™ may cause excessive engine wear.

Remember to always wear your seat belt while driving and shaving!

With Autoccino™ you never have to settle for lousy roadside coffee again.

A few years ago, Italy's Fiat Motor Company had a problem. Year after year, company employees were wrecking the latest models on the Italian Autobahn. The reason? These Fiat execs were driving 180 kilometers an hour after polishing off a couple of bottles of Monta Rosa rouge over lunch. A little drowsiness and before they knew it—boom! Fiat was out another 60,000,000 Lira.

The solution? Autoccino™—the world's finest in-vehicle caffeinated beverage brewing system.

No more antifreeze aftertaste.

If you've ever used a conventional automotive coffee maker, you know how easily that tangy antifreeze aftertaste can spoil a fine cup of coffee. With Autoccino™, though, you're guaranteed a great tasting cup of java, because those old-fashioned, leaky percolator-radiator interfaces have been completely eliminated. Autoccino™ uses a specially formulated milk product which actually *replaces* the antifreeze in your car. This antifreeze substitute constantly circulates around your vehicle's engine block, giving you a steaming hot cup of high test on demand—with no fussing and no waiting.

Five steps to better highway brewing.

Using our simplified, five-step installation manual, Autoccino™ can be installed under the hood of virtually any automobile in less than thirty minutes. Simply drain your car's radiator of any antifreeze (please flush thoroughly!), and bolt the Autoccino™ heat exchanger unit between your car's radiator and the engine block coolant return hose. Then fill your vehicle's radiator with Autoccino™'s Specially Formulated Milk, and you're on your way to great tasting coffee on the road.

Use the dash-mounted five-position knob to select from *ESPRESSO, SINGLE* or *DOUBLE CAFE LATTE, CAFE AMERICAN,* and Fiat's own rich Italian *BLACKTOP BREW.* After five cups of coffee, we recommend topping off the radiator when you make your next restroom stop.

Autoccino™ owners with turbo-equipped vehicles can request the Turbo Grinder™, at no additional cost. Turbo Grinder™ fits inside the turbo unit of your vehicle, grinding fresh beans on demand. (Please note that Turbo Grinder™ may void some auto warranties. Please check before installing.)

Thanks to Autoccino™, staying alert when you're on the road has never been easier.

- **Autoccino™ Automobile Coffee Brewer**
  #AWFLCFFE **$295.95 (17.50)**
- **Specially Formulated Milk/Antifreeze** (5 Gal)
  #MOOFRZE **$14.95 (5.00)**

MORE MR. MOTORHEAD

SPEND SOME MONEY.
RIGHT NOW.

A picture frame that ages your pictures gracefully, naturally.

How many times have you changed the pictures in your picture frames? Keeping up with the aging of friends and relatives can mean changing photos once every two or three years. Over the course of a lifetime, the amount of money you spend taking these new photos of your friends, and the valuable time lost replacing these pictures, is simply incalculable.

Thanks to the fine work of the researchers at the Alternative Applications Unit of Black Flag, the nationally recognized manufacturer of pest control gasses, you never have to change another photo again! These researchers have developed a unique solution to this endless and tiresome routine of changing photos: Ageous Gaseous™, an essentially harmless gas which slowly and naturally ages your pictures. Ageous™ does more than age the photographic paper—over many years, this time-released gas *actually ages the individuals in the photo.*

How does it work? The fact is, no one really knows for sure. Like so many other important scientific discoveries, the uncovering of Ageous™' properties was the result of an unintentional laboratory incident involving several chemical compounds.

Choose from brass, oak, or hand finished mahogany, in either 5"x7" or 8"x10" formats. Each frame comes with a rear-mounted Ageous™ canister, automatically calibrated to release its contents over forty years.

- **Ageous Gaseous™ Picture Frames**
  #BSFRM **$89.95 (6.50)**
  (Specify Style & Size)

Do not place Ageous Gaseous™ Picture Frames near frequently used areas such as desks or counter tops. Ageous™ gas is highly explosive and should only be used in well-ventilated areas!

Photo as it appears today in your Ageous Gaseous™ Picture Frame.

Same photo, 40 years later.

To order, call while sneezing

1-800-AH-AH-CHOO

Reach out and touch someone with our Wireless Telephone Stun Gun.™

With The Cutting Edge's Wireless Telephone Stun Gun™, now you have two ways to reach out and touch someone.

The phone portion of this phone stun gun features high-clarity, ten-channel digital transmission, assuring you of interference-free communications up to 2,000 feet away from the base unit. But wait—are you suddenly being approached by a potential assailant while you're on a call? Depress the *HOLD AND DEFEND* button, and you'll soon understand why this phone is a world apart from traditional cordless phones. Your call is automatically put on hold (music included!), as your phone's patented top-mounted elektroblastr™ beam comes to a full charge in less than three seconds. Reach out and touch someone, and they'll get the message—loud and clear.

At the high power *KO!* setting, your telephone delivers a 20,000 volt punch that causes involuntary contraction of the assailant's skeletal musculature. Not out to make such a high-voltage statement? Choose the low impact *STUN* or the mild attention getting *JOLT* for less serious threats. You can even dial down below the 200 volt *JOLT* setting—perfect for use on persons under 90 pounds or family pets.

Our Wireless Telephone Stun Gun™ runs on three rechargeable lead acid cells, good for three blasts when fully charged.

A Cutting Edge exclusive.

- **Wireless Telephone Stun Gun**™
#MKMYDY **$395.95 (15.00)**

STUPID LITTLE THINGS

Not just another paper clip.

Made from titanium-enhanced iron ore, Porsche Paper Clips™ maintain th clipping ability under the most adverse conditions. Special patented "spring-ba action insures smooth operation time after time. Here is a paper clip that's at in the boardroom, holding a 20-page legal brief together, or in the kitchen mak short work of an unwieldy stack of grocery coupons.

Endorsed by the American Office Products Association of America, these clips are available in limited edition sets of three. Elegant monogrammed lambskin over leather pouch holds your clips safely and securely when not in use.

Our titanium-enhanced iron ore Porsche Paper Clips™ come with a lifetime guarantee. If at any time these paper clips drop even *one paper*, return them for a full refund.

- **Porsche Paper Clips™ (Set of 3)**
  #WHTSTHEBGDL? $19.95 (1.00)

Melt stress away in your butt with Bunmatic Massage Briefcase.™

Anyone who's had to endure endless hours of anxiety ridden meetings knows how stress can concentrate itself in your butt. Like the neck and lower back, the derriere can be a focal point for stress. But if you're lucky enough to have a Bunmatic Massage Briefcase™, you're ready to melt away distracting rear-based stress on a moment's notice.

Ready for a powerful bun-shaking massage? Flip open Bunmatic™ and enter your weight, the duration of massage, and desired intensity (from *1* to *10* on Bunmatic's BunRichter™ scale) on the internal control pad. Reel out and plug in the AC power cord, close Bunmatic™'s top, and park your tired, stressed-out rear on the non-skid rubberized surface. When Bunmatic™'s weight sensor automatically detects that you're in position and ready for some relief, the three HP motor starts in with over 500 powerful gyrations per minute. Bunmatic™ uses the very same direct-drive motor as many industrial floor-washing units, eliminating the unreliable drive belts and pulley systems of other brands.

Butt wait—there's more.

Bunmatic™ is more than a professional quality massage device—it's also one of the most handsome briefcases on the market today. The briefcase portion of Bunmatic™ features supple, top-grain South American cowhide. Gold-plated hardware and a key-based locking system assure years of reliable service.

Use by persons over 300 pounds may cause permanent motor damage, possibly fire. Weighs 17 pounds.

- **Bunmatic Massage Briefcase™**
  #SHAKITUP **$89.95 (15.00)**

Sorry,  *delivery only.*

Time to floss!

A recent study from the American Dental Association found overwhelming evidence that after-dinner flossing is the single most neglected part of our daily oral hygiene. Thankfully, now there's Floss Swatch™ —a new way to assure a high level of personal oral hygiene, wherever you are.

Floss Swatch™ is more than just a dental aid—it's also a high-quality timepiece that features Swiss-style six-jewel movement that's accurate to eight minutes per day. Concealed under the stainless steel back cover is a spring-loaded spool wound with 50 feet of high tensile strength ADA-approved dental floss. Plus, each time you unwind a length of floss, a miniature bottom-mounted gear winds up the timepiece!

Your Floss Swatch™ watch comes with enough floss for twenty flossings. Order additional floss spools separately.

- **Floss Swatch™ Watch** #TME2FLOS **$45.95** **(3.50)**
- **Floss Spools** (Specify *Mint, Spicy Cinnamon*, or *Tequila* when ordering) #NEDMRFLS **$5.00** **(2.00)**

The science of making change revealed.

The quick way through tolls is the exact change lane, and CompuChange™ is the quick way to make change—quickly.

Punch in the amount of the toll in dollars and cents. *1 Dollar, 75 Cents.* Using its advanced microcircuitry design, CompuChange™ goes right to work indicating one possible change combination. *4 Quarters, 5 Dimes, 5 Nickels.* Hit *MU (MONEY UP)* and an alternate change combination is displayed. *2 Quarters, 12 Dimes, 5 Pennies.* Continue your search until you've located a change combination that you have in your possession. Typical toll booth amounts have literally *thousands* of change permutations. And CompuChange™ will display each and every one at your command.

CompuChange™ helps you make change at highway entrances and exits, bridges, and tunnels. You can even use it at parking garages.

Order today, and you'll never wait for change again.

- **CompuChange™** #MSTBKDING **$29.95 (3.50)**

To order, call while bungee jumping

1-800-BE-BOP-A-LU-LA

Finally. A golf shoe that gets you *and* the ball closer to the hole.

Here's a product that will improve your golf game dramatically, and *it's as easy as changing your shoes.*

The principle behind AdvantageYou™ Golf Shoes is simple. A recessed, concave aperture is built into the tip of the sole of AdvantageYou™'s right foot. All you do is locate your ball out on the course and discreetly step onto the golf ball, placing all of your body weight directly over the ball. A spring-loaded C-clamp locks down tight on the ball, securing it safely and unobtrusively to the shoe. From there on, the rest is up to you! Walk as far as you like—a few feet, or a hundred yards, or more—it doesn't matter. When it's time to release, just tap the heel of your right foot with a club. A hidden lever releases the golf ball and automatically resets the C-clamp.

AdvantageYou™'s are not a cheap pair of trick shoes. Made of durable Italian cowhide, AdvantageYou™'s feature a comfortable, breathable, and odor resistant cambrelle lining and black, rubberized soles with sure-grip cleats.

While not endorsed by golf professionals, AdvantageYou™ Golf Shoes are undoubtedly used by many. Get a pair today, and take 20 stokes off your score tomorrow!

■ **AdvantageYou™ Golf Shoes** #WEWNTTELL **$65.95 (6.00)**

Please note that right shoe weighs five pounds.

THE GAME YOU LOVE TO HATE

Top-Flite's briefcase combines good looks with super durability.

One glance at the Golfamania™ Briefcase is all it takes to know that you're someone who's serious about your golf. Very serious. After all, who else would travel with a briefcase that features more than eighty Top-Flite golf balls securely epoxied to the exterior?

Top-Flite's Golfamania™ Briefcase is more than a powerful statement—it's also one of the finest briefcases around, at any price. On the outside, golf balls provide permanent, hardened protection against every conceivable abuse. On the inside you'll find plenty of room for all your papers, with felt-lined surfaces throughout. There's even space for golf tees and golf balls!

Golfamania™ from Top-Flite. The perfect gift for the linkster in your life.

■ **Golfamania™ Briefcase** #BOZOBRFCSE **$79.95 (10.00)**

Golf NightScope™.

Have you ever wanted to play the truly great golf courses of the world, but didn't want the hassle of rearranging your portfolio so you could come up with an extra 50 grand for the initiation fee? If your answer is "yes," then Golf NightScope™ has the high-tech answer for you.

To use Golf NightScope™, settle the scope over the bridge of your nose, cinch down the adjustable head strap, and flip the scope to *ON*. The night will light up with a luminosity equivalent to 12,000 candlepower—almost the light levels of high noon. With Golf NightScope™, you can hit the links anytime from sundown to sunup—and it won't cost you a penny.

Our Golf NightScope™ incorporates advanced military-specification electronics, recently declassified from Operation Desert Storm's elite Covert Nocturnal Operations Forces. And with built-in military style features like a continuous distance readout and motion alarms, night golf will be so pleasurable you'll never want to play during the day again!

Endorsed by Arnold Palmer.

Our Golf NightScope™ is endorsed by veteran golf pro and four-time Masters champion Arnold Palmer. In fact, Arnie likes the NightScope™ so much he swears he's never going back to daytime golfing again!

■ **Golf NightScope™** #MDNITEDRV **$799.95 (12.50)**

To order, call real loud

1-800-OVER-HERE

Swiss Army Driver™.

Leave it to the Swiss to come up with a product as ingenious as the Swiss Army Driver™. Who else would have even thought that over thirty tools could be conveniently tucked away into the head of a driver?

Unscrew the removable mahogany and titanium head, and you'll find a veritable cache of handy instruments, from a thirteen-piece screwdriver set, to an array of six knives. There's even a snake bite kit just in case you have more trouble in the bunker than you had anticipated. Sure, this assortment of tools and equipment adds a few extra pounds to the driver, but we're confident that you'll find the extra weight is more than offset by the peace of mind that comes with owning the only golf driver given the seal of approval by the Los Angeles Police Department.

■ **Swiss Army Driver™** #EVRYTHNGBTKTCHNSNK **$399.95 (8.50)**

"Swiss Army Driver™'s plastique explosives cleanly removed a large boulder and several trees that were in my lie. Without this driver I never would have birdied the 18th hole at last year's P.G.A. Championship. This driver is so darn useful I carry it with me wherever I go—on and off the course." –John Daly

Burning calories takes on a whole new meaning with our HotWalker Treadmill.™

Throughout the ages, fire has a proven track record as a remarkable motivator. Remember the tens of thousands of ancient Romans who fled dozens of miles at top speed to escape the flames and lava of an erupting Mount Vesuvius? Or how about the coal walkers of Borneo, who endure years of rigorous training, knowing that they will someday have to confront the awesome heat of sizzling beds of coal. Today, though, there's no need to wait for a natural disaster or endure years of intense training to enjoy the full benefits of a heat-motivated workout.

Select the workout that's right for you.

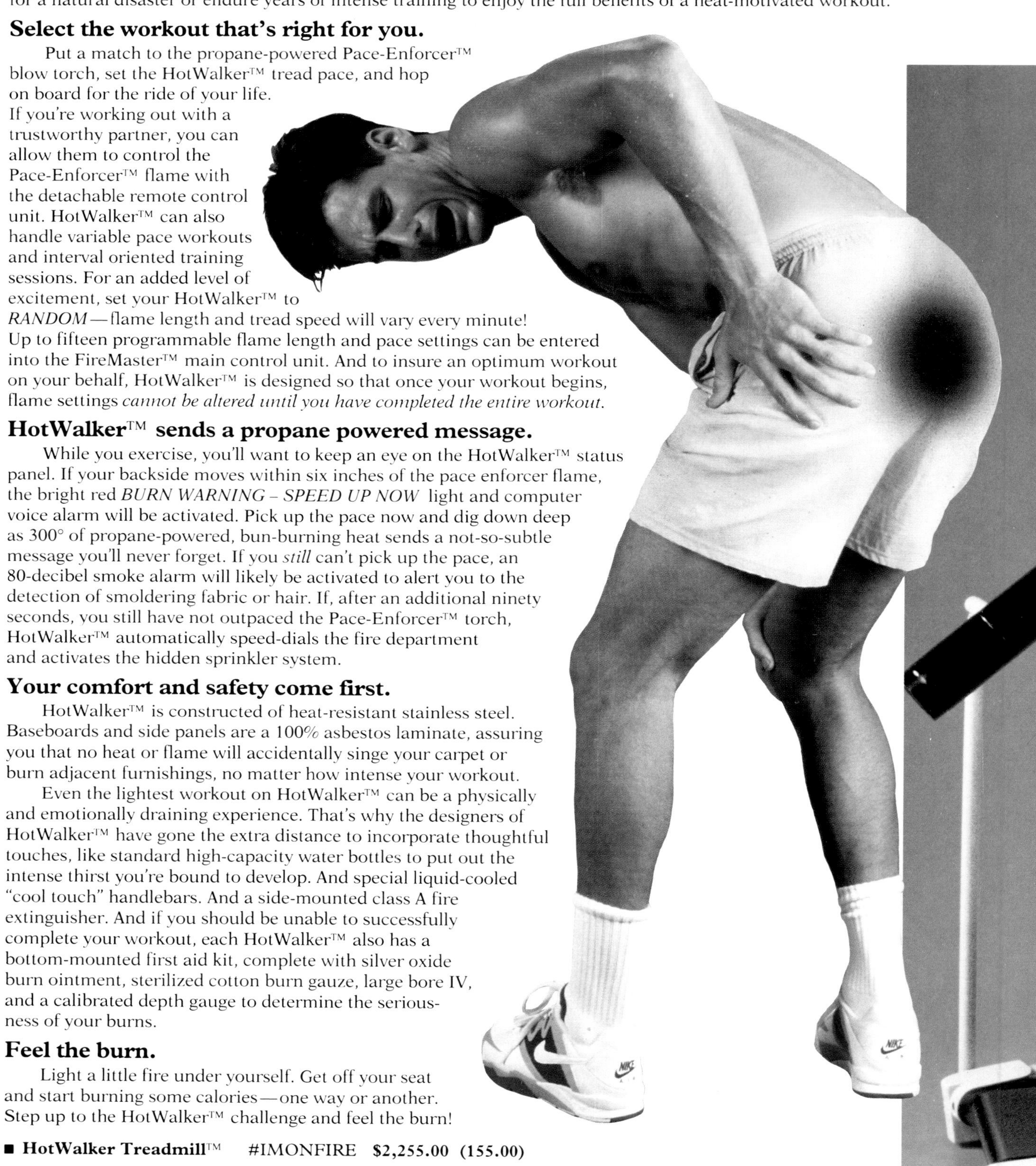

Put a match to the propane-powered Pace-Enforcer™ blow torch, set the HotWalker™ tread pace, and hop on board for the ride of your life. If you're working out with a trustworthy partner, you can allow them to control the Pace-Enforcer™ flame with the detachable remote control unit. HotWalker™ can also handle variable pace workouts and interval oriented training sessions. For an added level of excitement, set your HotWalker™ to *RANDOM*—flame length and tread speed will vary every minute! Up to fifteen programmable flame length and pace settings can be entered into the FireMaster™ main control unit. And to insure an optimum workout on your behalf, HotWalker™ is designed so that once your workout begins, flame settings *cannot be altered until you have completed the entire workout.*

HotWalker™ sends a propane powered message.

While you exercise, you'll want to keep an eye on the HotWalker™ status panel. If your backside moves within six inches of the pace enforcer flame, the bright red *BURN WARNING – SPEED UP NOW* light and computer voice alarm will be activated. Pick up the pace now and dig down deep as 300° of propane-powered, bun-burning heat sends a not-so-subtle message you'll never forget. If you *still* can't pick up the pace, an 80-decibel smoke alarm will likely be activated to alert you to the detection of smoldering fabric or hair. If, after an additional ninety seconds, you still have not outpaced the Pace-Enforcer™ torch, HotWalker™ automatically speed-dials the fire department and activates the hidden sprinkler system.

Your comfort and safety come first.

HotWalker™ is constructed of heat-resistant stainless steel. Baseboards and side panels are a 100% asbestos laminate, assuring you that no heat or flame will accidentally singe your carpet or burn adjacent furnishings, no matter how intense your workout.

Even the lightest workout on HotWalker™ can be a physically and emotionally draining experience. That's why the designers of HotWalker™ have gone the extra distance to incorporate thoughtful touches, like standard high-capacity water bottles to put out the intense thirst you're bound to develop. And special liquid-cooled "cool touch" handlebars. And a side-mounted class A fire extinguisher. And if you should be unable to successfully complete your workout, each HotWalker™ also has a bottom-mounted first aid kit, complete with silver oxide burn ointment, sterilized cotton burn gauze, large bore IV, and a calibrated depth gauge to determine the seriousness of your burns.

Feel the burn.

Light a little fire under yourself. Get off your seat and start burning some calories—one way or another. Step up to the HotWalker™ challenge and feel the burn!

■ **HotWalker Treadmill™** #IMONFIRE **$2,255.00 (155.00)**

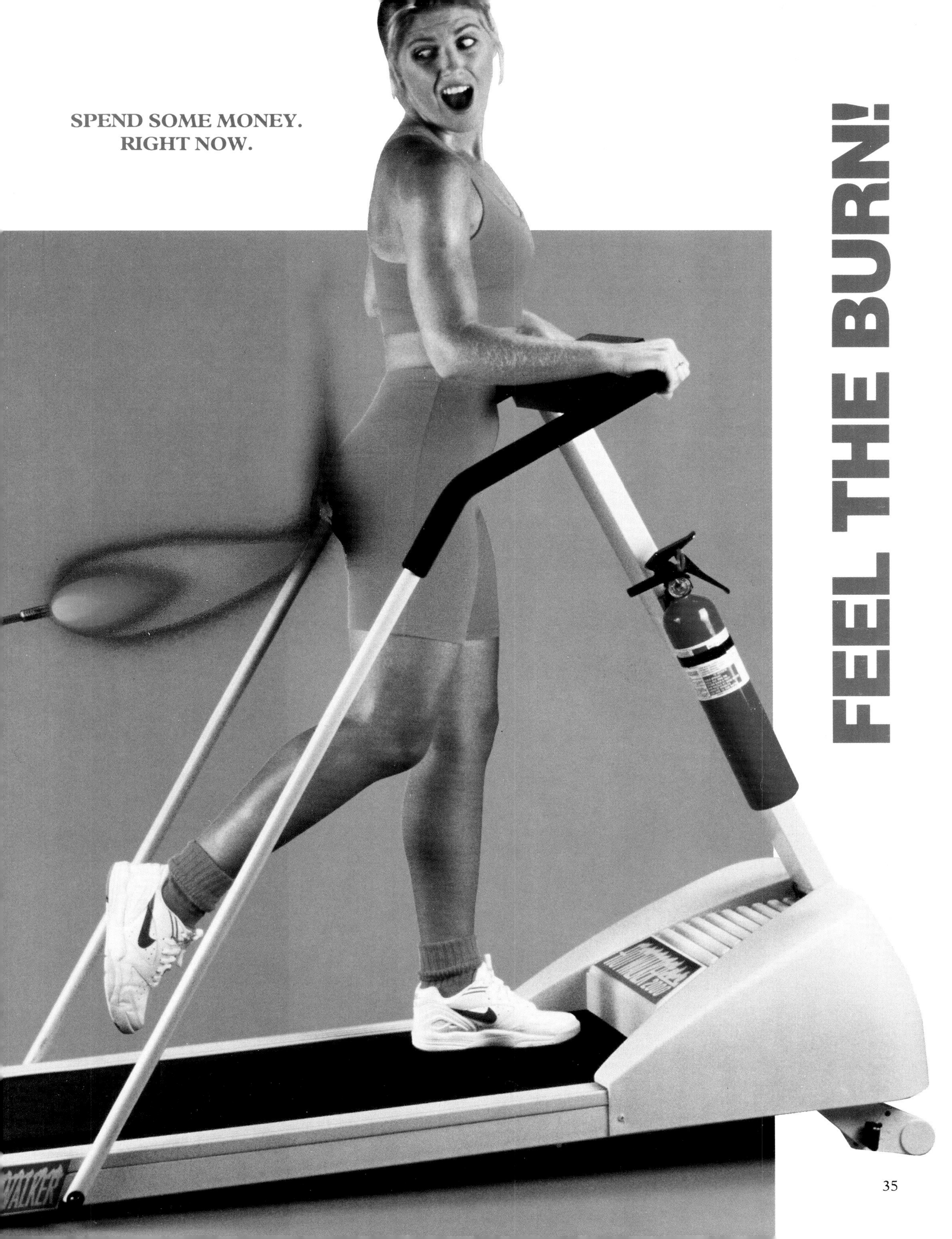
SPEND SOME MONEY.
RIGHT NOW.
FEEL THE BURN!

Catch Cat!™
Nintendo's answer to Fido's long days at home.

Do your canine friend a favor, and add a whole new world of excitement to long, monotonous days alone at home. Designed by world-famous Nintendo, Catch Cat!™ is the world's first interactive video entertainment system designed specifically for canine use.

Because Catch Cat!™ is designed with the canine user in mind, your dog will understand the controls and objective almost immediately. Eighteen levels of cat chasing, beginning with the lawn sequence and culminating in the doghouse feline death trap, assures that it will take Fido many weeks to finally catch the cat! A special paw-assist keyboard makes Catch Cat!™ easy to operate. Ultra-high frequency cat noises are played over the internal speaker, keeping Fido intensely focused on the game at hand. The exciting pre-programmed audio soundtrack includes realistic cat screeches, meows, and genuine cat fight noises.

Six user-selectable degrees of difficulty range from *IRISH SETTER* mode for less intelligent dogs, to *TERRIER & MUTT* for cunning or street-smart canines. Catch Cat!™ includes scratch-proof keyboard and slobber-resistant screen.

■ **Catch Cat!™** #MEOWWOOFWOOF! **$499.95 (35.00)**

Dog Stockings.™ Our most popular product ever.

We first put Dog Stockings™ in our catalog on a whim. The response was unbelievable. We were sold out in less than a week. The following year we ordered ten times the quantity. And we sold out in three weeks. This year, we've ordered 800,000 Dog Stockings™. We hope it's enough.

A dog in a stocking is worth two on a leash.

With Dog Stocking™, carrying your best friend around town is no problem. Just slide Fido into the form-fitting acrylic stocking (tail end first!), cinch the drawstring (not too tight!), and you're on your way. Once you're home, hang Fido up for a nap and you can rest, confident that he's keeping his nose out of trouble. Once you own a pair of Dog Stockings™, you'll wonder how you ever survived without them.

Dog Stockings™ are made from a durable, colorful acrylic and feature an odor- and stain-resistant synthetic lining. Endorsed by noted canine expert Dr. Karl von Schlemp of the American Kennel Club. Used by more than 1,000 kennels nationwide. One size fits all.

■ **Dog Stocking™** #K9STUFFIT **$17.95 (5.00)**

Learn the thrilling, sensual touch of the American Kennel Club.

Most of us think that petting a dog is no big deal—fast or slow, ears or tummy—it doesn't really matter where or how you pet your canine friend. Right? Wrong! Your pet knows the difference, and sometimes only a few inches here or there can mean the difference between unadulterated bliss and unfathomable canine remorse.

Working with the world's foremost canine masseur, the American Kennel Club's Dr. Karl von Schlemp, The Cutting Edge has developed two four-hour instructional videos. Dr. von Schlemp starts at the muzzle and covers over 300 canine body parts, including the occiput (head), flews, brisket, pastern, loin, thigh, and hock, and concluding with the rump and tail.

The elusive "K9" spot, the nine fur zones, and the Karma Dogma.

You may not realize it, but each breed responds differently to canine massage therapy. Dr. von Schlemp will show you unique techniques for each breed, from the sensual St. Bernard tummy rub, to the invigorating Black Lab ear scratch. He even covers detailed information on determining the location of the elusive "K9 Hot Spot" for your breed. Plus, Dr. von Schlemp details the nine fur zones and discusses some of the implications of the provocative Karma Dogma techniques.

Please specify short or long hair when ordering. These VHS color videos are for sale to adults only (canine models are nude). Let Dr. von Schlemp help you say "thank you" to your pet for all those years of unwavering loyalty. Order today.

- **Secrets of Pet Massage Video (short hair)**
  #HPYDG1 **$35.95 (2.50)**
- **Secrets of Pet Massage Video (long hair)**
  #HPYDG2 **$35.95 (2.50)**

To order, fetch phone, bark, slobber and call

1-800-GOODBOY-GOODBOY

To order, don't even bother to call

1-800-WHAT-A-JERK

FOR THE PUTZ IN YOUR LIFE

"Waiter, I believe this Merlot is a trifle fruity on the upper palate."

"Est le vin to your liking, Monsieur?" For many of us, those are words that strike dread into our hearts. After all, to achieve a truly discriminating sense for wine takes years of refinement, development, and a lot of drinking. Until now.

Silicon Valley meets the Rhone Valley.

Using VinNez™ is a snap. Simply mount VinNez™ over your nose and lower the bio-mechanical nose to the wine surface. When you press *SNIFF ON,* VinNez™'s bio-receptor sensors go to work. First, airborne wine molecules are sucked into VinNez™'s nasal chambers. Here, artificial olfactory cells receive and categorize individual organic molecules. VinNez™'s bio-electronic brain then interprets this raw data, and relays this information to the patented "Jacques Le Vin" software program—named for the late French wine taster, whose nose was used as the basis for VinNez™'s proprietary interpretative program. To read the results of your wine study, lift the VinNez™ glasses off your face and glance casually at the micro LCD display that is imbedded in the upper nasal passages.

Order VinNez™ today, and put those snotty French waiters in their place tomorrow.

- **VinNez™**
  #SNOTNOSE **$194.95 (10.00)**
- **Replacement Nose Hairs**
  #HAIRS **$99.95 (5.00)**

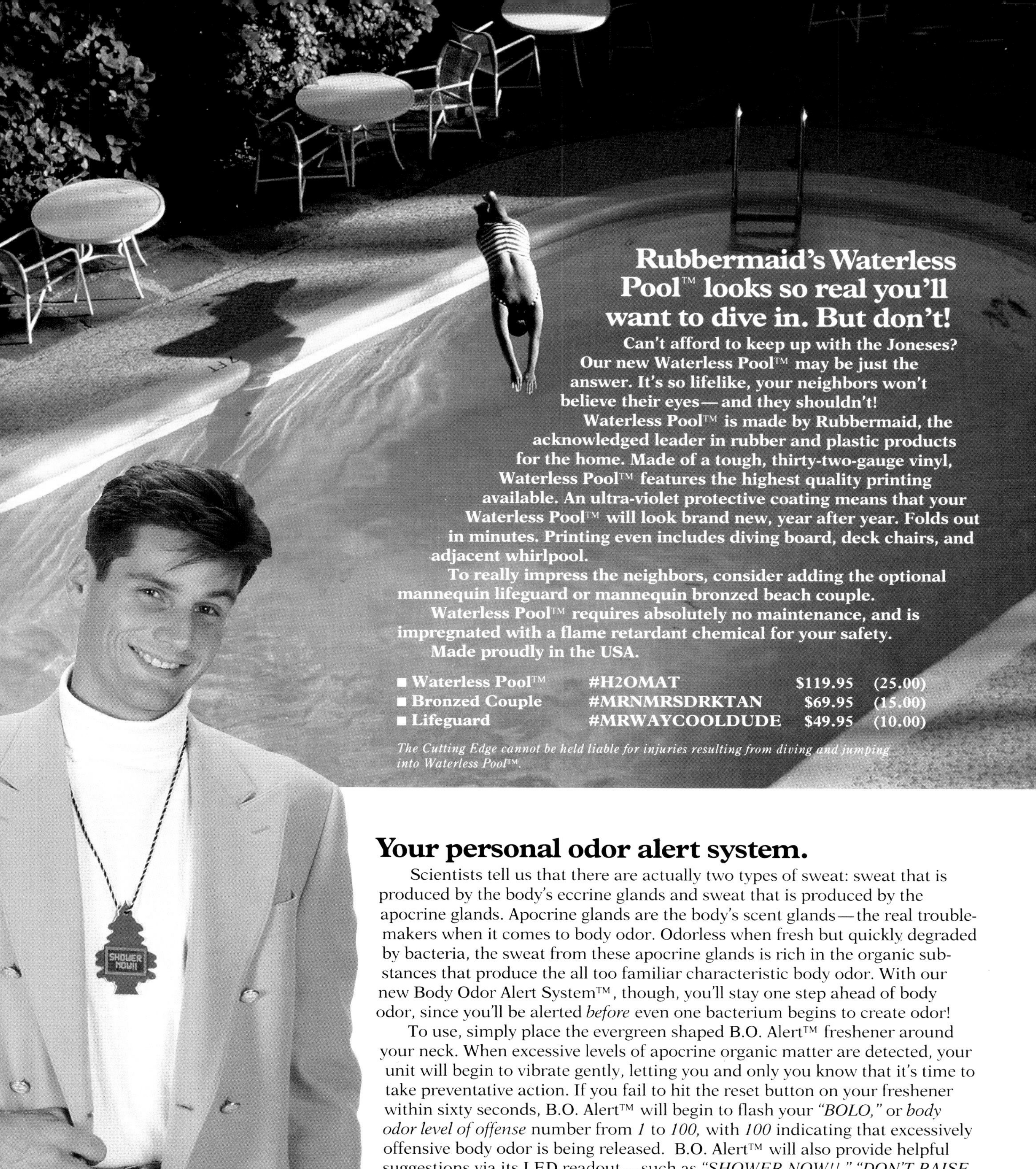

Rubbermaid's Waterless Pool™ looks so real you'll want to dive in. But don't!

Can't afford to keep up with the Joneses? Our new Waterless Pool™ may be just the answer. It's so lifelike, your neighbors won't believe their eyes—and they shouldn't!

Waterless Pool™ is made by Rubbermaid, the acknowledged leader in rubber and plastic products for the home. Made of a tough, thirty-two-gauge vinyl, Waterless Pool™ features the highest quality printing available. An ultra-violet protective coating means that your Waterless Pool™ will look brand new, year after year. Folds out in minutes. Printing even includes diving board, deck chairs, and adjacent whirlpool.

To really impress the neighbors, consider adding the optional mannequin lifeguard or mannequin bronzed beach couple.

Waterless Pool™ requires absolutely no maintenance, and is impregnated with a flame retardant chemical for your safety.

Made proudly in the USA.

- **Waterless Pool™ #H2OMAT $119.95 (25.00)**
- **Bronzed Couple #MRNMRSDRKTAN $69.95 (15.00)**
- **Lifeguard #MRWAYCOOLDUDE $49.95 (10.00)**

The Cutting Edge cannot be held liable for injuries resulting from diving and jumping into Waterless Pool™.

Your personal odor alert system.

Scientists tell us that there are actually two types of sweat: sweat that is produced by the body's eccrine glands and sweat that is produced by the apocrine glands. Apocrine glands are the body's scent glands—the real trouble-makers when it comes to body odor. Odorless when fresh but quickly degraded by bacteria, the sweat from these apocrine glands is rich in the organic substances that produce the all too familiar characteristic body odor. With our new Body Odor Alert System™, though, you'll stay one step ahead of body odor, since you'll be alerted *before* even one bacterium begins to create odor!

To use, simply place the evergreen shaped B.O. Alert™ freshener around your neck. When excessive levels of apocrine organic matter are detected, your unit will begin to vibrate gently, letting you and only you know that it's time to take preventative action. If you fail to hit the reset button on your freshener within sixty seconds, B.O. Alert™ will begin to flash your *"BOLO,"* or *body odor level of offense* number from *1* to *100,* with *100* indicating that excessively offensive body odor is being released. B.O. Alert™ will also provide helpful suggestions via its LED readout—such as *"SHOWER NOW!!," "DON'T RAISE ARMS!!,"* and others. And with a pleasing evergreen scent automatically released from your pendant whenever readings over 50 are detected, you know you've got your bases covered.

Order your Body Odor Alert System™ today. Because nobody should let their personal body odor get in the way of the sweet smell of success.

- **Body Odor Alert System™** #PUALERT **$149.95 (5.00)**

Use during heavy physical exercise may cause unit to permanently malfunction. Such use voids warranty.

I
FEEL
MELLOW
IF YOU DON'T
NEED IT,
MAYBE
SOMEONE ELSE
WILL.
Medium Rock of
the Gods™
The lovely temple
and gardens at Kyoto
from which we get
the rocks.

Ancient Japanese stress remedy. The Shinto Rock of the Gods.™

Shinto monks are probably the most relaxed people anywhere in the world. These diminutive, gentle souls have redefined the word "mellow." How is it that these kind monks can achieve and maintain such intense states of relaxation? Is it the soothing atmosphere of the monastery? The low-key lifestyle? We had to know.

But getting these inscrutable little guys to talk wasn't so easy. They weren't even interested in money! Only in the last year, and after months of fruitless attempts, have these shy monks finally disclosed their innovative stress reduction technique.

Soothing micro-granitic protrusions.

The secret? A rock! But not just any old rock. Look closely at the Shinto Rock of the Gods™ and you'll begin to notice that the surface of the Rock of the Gods™ is not smooth at all. In fact, it has literally thousands of tiny granite protrusions—protrusions that go to work, relaxing tense skin surfaces and sending a soothing, radiating ripple into deeper skin tissues.

The Shinto monks massage their Rock of the Gods™ for several minutes during morning prayers. But you can use yours whenever and wherever you want. Whether you're at the office on the phone with an important client, or at home in the midst of preparing a gourmet dinner for twenty, this rock will help keep you calm, cool, and collected. Just a few minutes a day with your Rock of the Gods™, and you'll feel like a new you!

From the Gardens of Kyoto to you.

This offer is limited to the first 1,000 customers, or until the Kyoto gardens are out of rocks, whichever comes first. For every rock order, The Cutting Edge will donate 60 cents to support the Shinto Monastery.

- **Rock of the Gods™: Small** #LTLRCK **$44.95 (5.00)**
- **Rock of the Gods™: Medium** #MEDRCK **$69.95 (6.00)**
- **Rock of the Gods™: Large** #BIGRCK **$99.95 (10.00)**

To order, meditate until achieving complete inner bliss and dial

1-800-NIRVANAAAAA

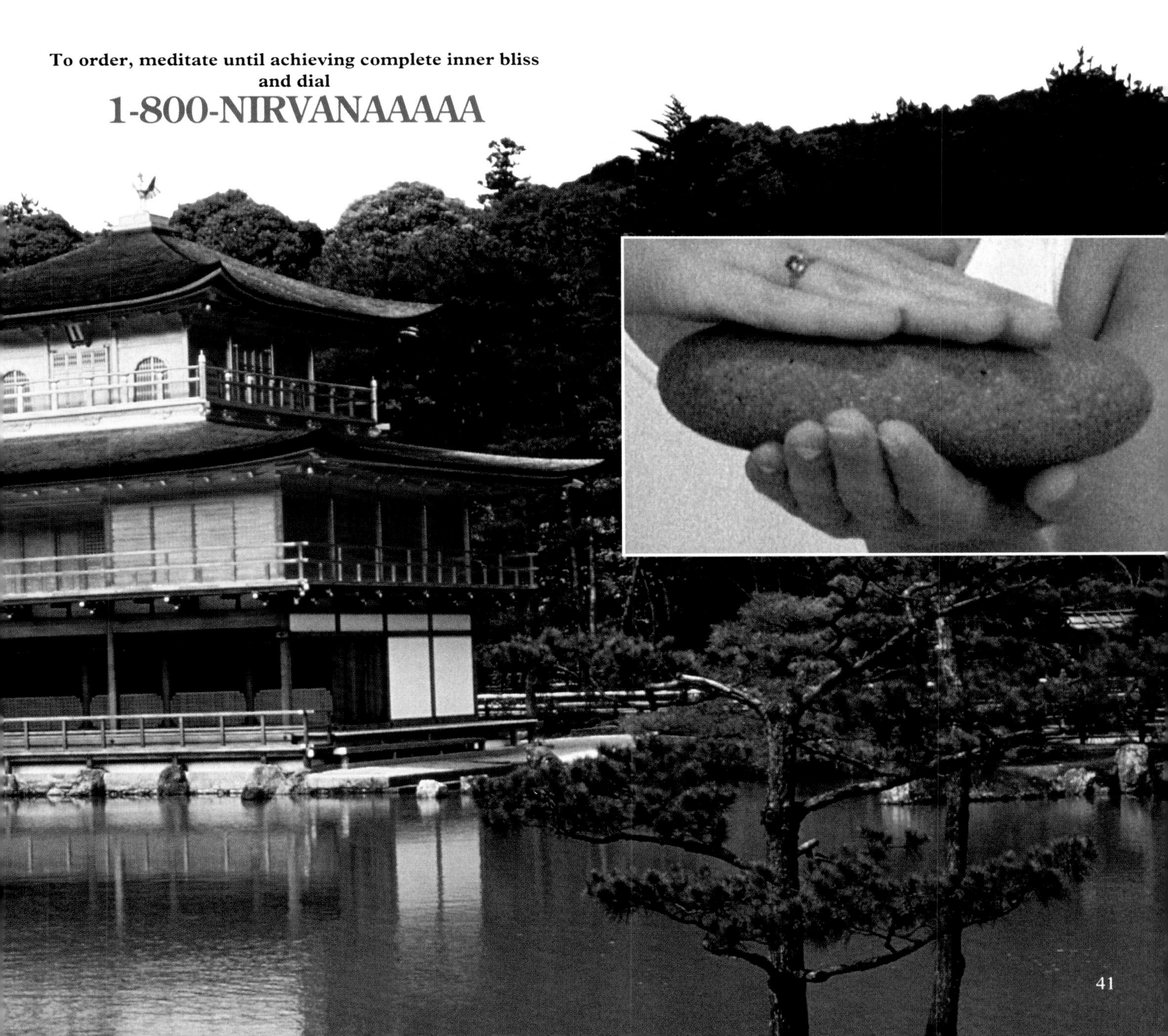

Give your brain a jump start. With Mr. Goodbrain.™

A professional colleague of ours had all kinds of problems with intense anxiety. He tried everything: audio tapes, massage, relaxation techniques, even exceptionally powerful medication. Nothing worked. Then we turned him on to Mr. Goodbrain™—literally! The results were shocking. In less than two weeks, he was relaxed—very, very relaxed. So relaxed, some of his skeletal muscles became permanently flaccid.

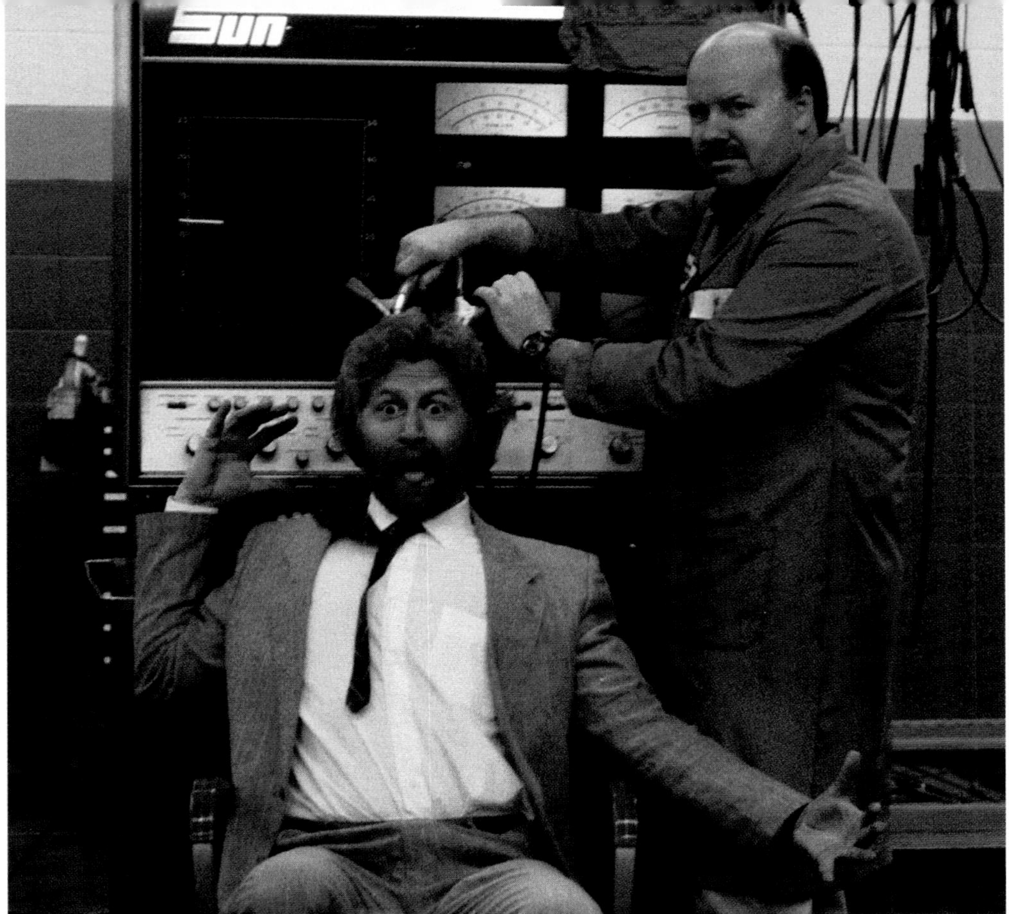

300 volts and the "Cerebral Reset Response."

What happens when the high-voltage clamps are attached to your temporal lobes and high frequency blasts of 300 volts are sent out? Not even the world's top neurosurgeons know for sure. What we think happens is that tiny bolts of lightning jump across the synapses of each of the 10 billion neurons that compose your nervous system. When this happens, all 10 billion neurons go off, or "fire," simultaneously. What does this mean for you? It's hard to say, *exactly*. But consider this comparison: it takes just *seven* neurons firing simultaneously to trigger a Grand Mal epileptic seizure.

What we do know for sure is that your tired, stressed out brain will likely respond with the "Cerebral Reset Response"—completely clearing your mind of virtually all undesirable thoughts and memories. When the power is turned off, you'll be left with a sense of relaxation so profound you may wonder if you're still alive.

A location near you.

With more than 100 locations nationwide, The Cutting Edge makes it easy for you to come by for a quick session before work. For stubborn cases of tension, consider the purchase of a home unit.

- **Mr. Goodbrain™: Coupon for One Session**
  #HEDFRY **$55.00** **(2.00)**
- **Mr. Goodbrain™ Home Unit**
  #HMEFRY **$7,455.00** **(255.00)**
- **Optional Body Restraints (recommended)**
  #HLDDWN **$89.95** **(15.00)**

The Cutting Edge is not responsible for intentional misuse. The Cutting Edge recommends that persons trained in cardiopulmonary resuscitation ("CPR") and advanced cardiac life support ("ACLS") be available during operation. Installation of a standard surge suppressor during operation is highly recommended. Feelings of disorientation, paranoia, and occasional memory loss may be experienced following treatment. If problems persist, we strongly recommend purchase of an Xtra Brain (Geraldo, Bob, or Spock) featured on page 6 in this catalog.

To order, don't call, we'll call you

1-800-KARNAK

Acu-Peck.™ New mechanical Miatsu bird pecks away at sore back muscles.

For more than six centuries, New Guinea tribesmen have known about the benefits of Miatsu bird massage. Placing honey-soaked baobab seeds on each other's backs, they would wait patiently for the shy Miatsu bird to land and begin pecking. Like magic, these precious little birds would peck *only on acupressure points on the body!* And because of the Miatsu bird, these rugged little tribesmen are the only culture in the world that are known to be *completely free* of back pain—so free that they don't even have an expression for it!

"Miatsusana Jujuwana!"

The tribesmen call it "Miatsusana Jujuwana," or "delightful pecking from the little red pecking bird." Since the turn of the century, Westerners with chronic back pain would attempt the dangerous voyage to Papua, New Guinea, to seek certain relief. Efforts to import this unique avian creature during the past several decades have always failed, as the frail little bird would invariably perish in transit. Today, however, we are able to offer a fully *mechanized* version of the Miatsu bird. And you don't have to call it "Miatsusana Jujuwana." You can call it "relief," pure and simple.

Just like the real thing.

Our mechanical Miatsu bird features a powerful beak that's precision rotomolded from a Kevlar mold. At full speed, the Miatsu beak generates over 75 pecks per minute. And, since each peck impacts the skin surface with more than 50 pounds per square inch of pinpoint pressure, tense, knotted back muscles will immediately begin to relax.

Endorsed by American Chiropractic Association, American Physical Therapy Association, and the Audubon Society.

Order a set of five Miatsu birds today and you'll say goodbye to chronic back pain for good!

- **Acu-Peck™ Miatsu Birds (Set of Five)**
  #JUJUWANA! **$129.95 (7.50)**

I FEEL VERY MELLOW

A TOUCH OF CLASS

Detail of Monet's "The Bridge At Argenteuil"

Monet . . . and me! Why just own a masterpiece when you can be in one?

Imagine the thrill of owning Van Gogh's "Starry Night" and looking very closely . . . only to find you and your special someone under the stars! Or perhaps you would rather own Monet's "The Bridge At Argenteuil," in which you and your wife can be seen out for a Sunday cruise in your new power boat.

Original-quality artistry.

The original masters knew what they were doing—those folks were super painters. And in order to lovingly recreate their creations, Great Masters & You has spared no expense. With scholarship work-study students from some of the finest art schools in the world behind the easel, you're assured that your painting will be a family heirloom for generations to come.

Tell us what you want . . . or let us surprise you!

All you do is send us a color photo of you and your family, with a detailed note on the backside of the photo indicating your desired placement and activity, such as "picnicking with Rebecca next to the rowboat," "swimming with my scuba gear under the bridge in the distance," or "riding my Harley on the dirt road by the river." We do the rest—in the exact style of the original masters. For an added surprise, forget the instructions and just send us a photo of your family. We'll get them all into the painting, one way or another.

Great Masters & You paintings are professionally framed in gold gilded-type frames. Just like the originals. Please allow six weeks for the creation of your masterpiece and its delivery—remembering that a craftsman can never be rushed at his craft.

Item	Code	Price	
■ **Van Gogh's "Starry Night"**	**#VGSTARS**	**$299.95**	**(25.00)**
■ **Monet's "The Bridge At Argenteuil"**	**#CMWATER**	**$299.95**	**(25.00)**
■ **Picasso's "Guernica"**	**#PPWAR**	**$299.95**	**(25.00)**

Artistry and nuclear waste meet in Half Life Sculptures.™

If you've ever worked in the control room of a nuclear power facility, you know how deathly boring this work can be. There's nothing to do. The plant runs itself, and when something goes wrong, there's not much you can do about it anyway. To combat the long hours of boredom in the control room, many operators have taken up the relatively new art form of sculpting spent fuel rods. Some of these artists work right through the night. And some of their creations are stunning, powerfully dramatic works of art.

Out of the plant and into your home.

The Cutting Edge is proud to offer our customers the opportunity to own these acclaimed Half Life Sculptures™. Each sculpture consists of at least three, twenty-foot rods of uranium 238 encased in a thin but super strong clear carbon fiber fuel sheath. Your Half Life Sculpture™ is installed on a genuine Italian marble stand, and is personally signed by the artist-operator. A personalized fact sheet accompanies each sculpture, giving information on the dates of use and plant location of your particular rods.

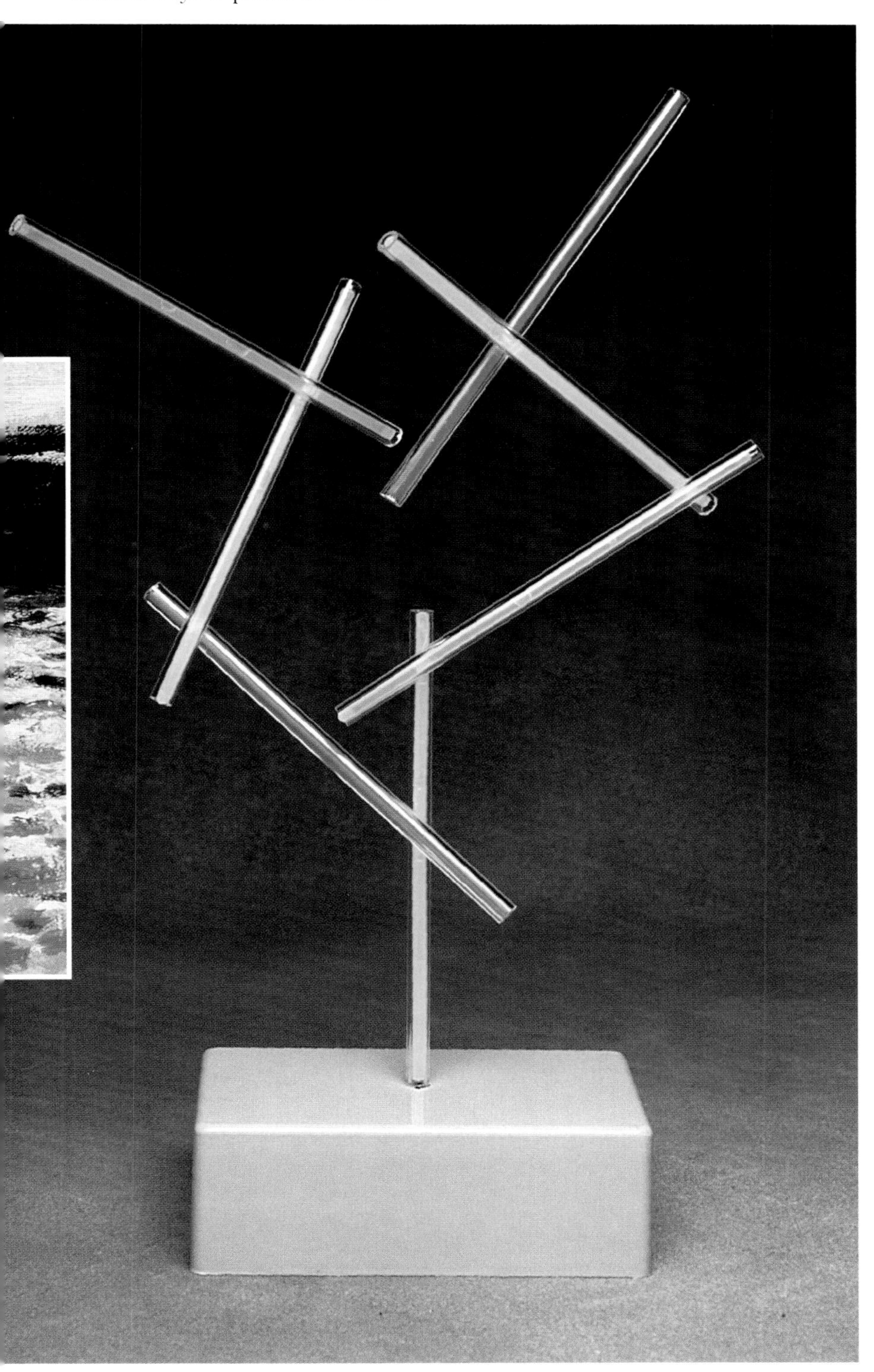

Watch it glow. And decay!

With Half Life Sculptures™ there's no need to worry about having to install specialized museum quality lighting, because all Half Life Sculptures™ glow on their own. All day, all night. The pleasing colored lights that radiate from your sculpture also provide several degrees of additional heat to the room. As the years go by, the glow will imperceptibly diminish—because your sculpture is actually transforming itself before your very eyes! Through the miracle of unstable isotopic decay, each Half Life Sculpture™ is slowly and steadily changing from uranium 238 into a harmless lead byproduct.

Each Half Life™ masterpiece is shipped with mandatory radiation alarms and must be delivered via DOE hazardous waste, level C radiation protocols. Not recommended for installation in children's rooms or food preparation areas. Cannot be shipped overseas.

■ **Half Life Sculpture**™
#MAYCSCNCR **$1,495.95 (7,500.00)**

Sorry,  *delivery of this item not available.*

To order, don't bother to call, just send cash to

1-800-AUTHORS-C/O-MACMILLAN-PUB-CO.

Interwax™ For brighter, cleaner, better hearing ears.

It's happened to all of us at one time or another—the boss pulls you aside for a confidential one-on-one, whispers an important detail in your ear, and rushes off to a closed-door meeting. Seconds later you realize you *didn't hear what he said*. A valuable piece of information is lost to earwax build up. More often than you might realize, earwax has stopped career advancement cold. But now you can put a stop to earwax build up for good. Introducing the Q-Tip for the Nineties: Interwax™.

5,000 pounds per square inch.

Interwax™ pulses a piping hot patented acidic cleaning solution down the auditory canal through its one hundred microjet heads. With over 5,000 PSI of scrubbing power, the acidic solution—which was first developed as an industrial cleaning solvent—easily pierces through the tympanic membrane to rout out wax before it can form. The hot solution settles on the cochlea in your inner ear as it individually scrubs each of the 20,000 sensory hair follicles for a deep-down clean. Additional cleaning down the Eustachian tube leaves your mouth feeling tingly clean. Some customers report that a thorough cleaning with Interwax™ makes use of their Interplak instrument all but unnecessary. Flick the switch and go from *FLUSH* to *SUCTION*, as you evacuate and dispose of dislodged inner ear waste material.

"Please, don't shout!"

After just a few cleanings, you can't help but notice the difference. Hearing improvements of several *hundred* decibels is not uncommon. Some customers report that they can actually hear through walls, even buildings.

So don't be left behind again. Climb right to the top of the corporate ladder with cleaner, better hearing ears. Order Interwax™ today.

- **Interwax™** #QUIETPLS **$89.95 (8.00)**
- **Micro Jet Replacement Head** #EARHDS **$49.95 (2.00)**

First-time users of Interwax™ should avoid all loud noises for up to 24 hours following cleaning. Sensations of dizziness and loss of balance may be experienced after use.

Laser-Razor™ takes the laser out of the laboratory and into the lavatory.

Can you imagine a shave so close that it rivals the precision of orthoscopic surgery? Now imagine a shaver so powerful it utilizes laser technology from the Star Wars weapons research program. Thanks to recent federal deregulation, we are able to use a 1500 watt yttrium-aluminum-garnet red light class 5 laser, the most powerful laser that civilians can own. (Permit required.) And with power like that, you're guaranteed a shave so close you'll think you'll never grow facial hairs again!

What happens when 1500 watts of laser power meets your facial skin?

With that kind of power, stubborn hair follicles are incinerated so completely and efficiently that barely a wisp of smoke is left behind. And Laser-Razor™ pierces deep—way down past the hair follicle into the subcutaneous skin layers, where hairs begin—to destroy the papilla, the center of hair growth. Laser-Razor™ gives you a shave that's guaranteed to be close—real close. How close is *real close?* So close that we have to use the scientific measurement unit of one angstrom. With Laser-Razor™, you'll get a shave that is a *minimum* of three angstroms close. And with one angstrom equalling one ten-billionth of a meter, you know that's awful darn close.

Experience the shave that's light years ahead of traditional technology. Experience the warm burning sensation of high-power laser technology. Experience Laser-Razor™.

- **Laser-Razor™**
  #WHSKERZAP **$595.95 (10.00)**

To order, call while sneezing

1-800-AH-AH-CHOO

HAVE YOU
CALLED
OUR
800 NUMBER
TODAY
TO SPEND
SOME MORE
MONEY?

Mr. Bigtime™ Watch is easy to read. REAL EASY.

IF YOU'RE ONE OF THE MILLIONS WHO SUFFERS FROM MYOPIA, HYPEROPIA, CATARACTS, GLAUCOMA, OR JUST CHRONICALLY BLURRY VISION, OUR EASY-TO-READ MR. BIGTIME™ WATCH MAY BE THE ONLY WATCH FOR YOU.

MR. BIGTIME™ WAS THE RESULT OF A LENGTHY RESEARCH PROJECT CONDUCTED BY THE AMERICAN OPTOMETRIC ASSOCIATION. UNIVERSITY RESEARCHERS DISCOVERED THAT THE SIMPLEST CORRECTIVE MEASURE FOR COUNTLESS VISION DEFICIENCIES WAS TO *MAKE THINGS BIGGER.*

THE SEVEN-INCH DIAMETER FACE ON MR. BIGTIME™ HAS MORE THAN FIFTY TIMES THE SURFACE AREA OF A TRADITIONAL WRISTWATCH, AND FEATURES OVER ONE-INCH HIGH NUMERALS. MR. BIGTIME™ RUNS ON FOUR D CELLS (NOT SUPPLIED), INCLUDES A HEAVY DUTY SEATBELT-STYLE WRIST BUCKLE, AND IS GUARANTEED TO BE ACCURATE TO WITHIN TEN MINUTES PER DAY. A REINFORCED PLASTIC CASE MAKES MR. BIGTIME™ LIGHTWEIGHT (UNDER FOUR POUNDS) AND STURDY. MR. BIGTIME™ IS NOT WATERPROOF.

IF YOU CAN'T READ MR. BIGTIME™, YOU'RE EITHER ASLEEP OR LEGALLY BLIND.

■ **MR. BIGTIME™** #HVYWRST **$34.95 (8.00)**

Power Tie™ Let the force be with you.

Here is the first necktie that can rightfully claim the name *power tie.*

Simply flip the concealed switch to *ON* and Power Tie™'s rotating hypnodisk™ comes up to full speed ever so slowly—so slowly, in fact, that no one ever notices it. Until it's too late, that is. By then, your corporate adversary will be so entranced, his center of attention will literally be "sucked in" to Power Tie™'s mesmerizing rotating hypnodisk™. In a matter of moments he'll be the mental equivalent of a fresh bowl of Jell-o.

For the person who has already "made up their mind," simply reverse the direction of rotation and repeat your request. For extra tough subjects, switch to *SUPER-HYPNODISK™* which delivers over 1800 rpm.

Endorsed by the American Psychological Association.

When the Board of Directors of the American Psychological Association saw our claims regarding Power Tie™, they dismissed the product as "complete quackery." But after a two-hour, closed-door meeting, we had them 100% convinced. In fact, Power Tie™ is wholeheartedly endorsed by every organization that has had an opportunity to meet with us, including Ralph Nader and the hard-to-please Consumer Reports. How did we do it? Take one guess.

■ **Power Tie™** #OBEYME **$39.95 (2.50)**

"Sorry, Bill, but I don't think this merger is meant to be."

Bad Deal Detector™ is worth its weight in gold.

You don't need to have a Ph.D. in computer science to use our new Bad Deal Detector™ from Sashimi, maker of fine consumer electronic products for over ten years. All it takes is three AA batteries and a willingness to be open-minded.

Before your next meeting starts, depress the *DEAL SENSE* button to activate your detector. As your deal progresses, Bad Deal Detector™ searches the conversation for critical business terminology and phraseology, locking on and analyzing key elements of the proposed deal. At the conclusion of your meeting, check the Bad Deal Detector™ meter, which gives you a range of response from *"YOU LOSE, THEY WIN," "YOU LOSE, THEY LOSE,"* to *"YOU WIN, THEY WIN,"* and, saving best for last, *"YOU WIN, THEY LOSE."*

Bad Deal Detector™ uses an advanced business algorithm, developed at the Harvard Business School, that compares your deal with over 100,000 national and international bad deals from over the past fifty years, including such famous bad deals as the purchase of People's Express Airline and the hostages-for-arms deal with Iran.

Imagine what Trump would have paid for this.

How much is Bad Deal Detector™ worth? If you were Donald Trump, it would have been worth its weight in gold. (Actually, more than 100 times its weight in gold for the Trump Casino deals alone.)

Priced at under $200, business' best friend is a "win-win" situation for you. Order Bad Deal Detector™ today and never go along with a bad deal again.

■ **Bad Deal Detector™** #NOWYITS4RL **$199.95 (7.50)**

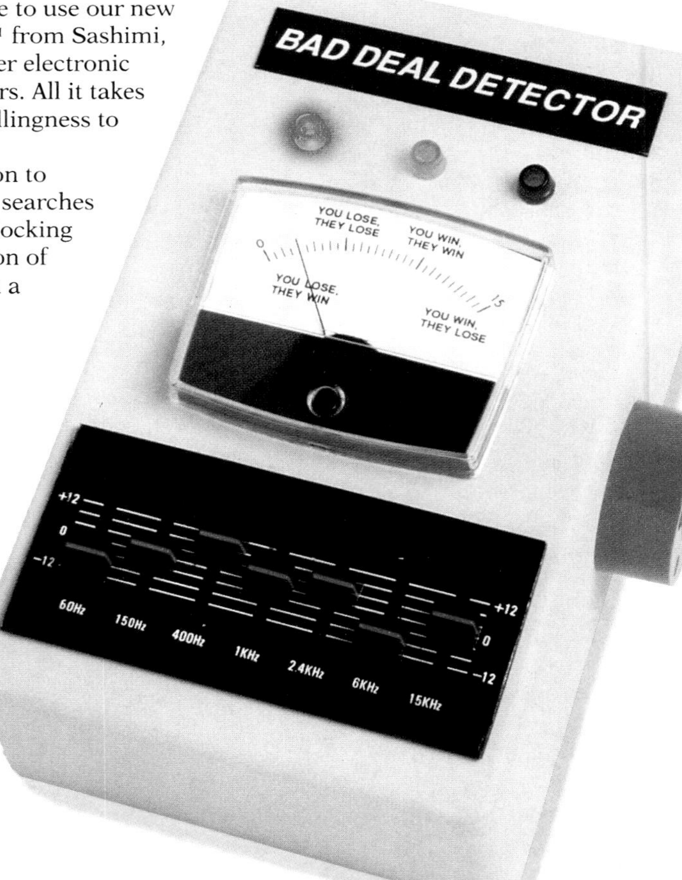

Burger™ takes the guess work out of lunch.

Teriyaki, a leader in high-tech pocket computing, makes going out to lunch a piece of cake with its powerful (128 megabyte) wide-screen, multi-function Burger™. Utilizing the same technology that helps steer supertankers safely back to port, Burger™ *triangulates* your position from orbiting satellites and then matches this information to its internal database of over one million fast-food establishments. And that means lunch. Fast.

"Burger, s'il vous plait."

French food is fine, if that's what you like, but sometimes only a burger will do. Lunchtime is rapidly approaching, but no need to worry. You have Burger™. Grab your Burger™ and punch in your cross-street coordinates. *Rue Saint Jacques* and *Champs Élysée.* Microseconds later Burger™ displays the name and location of each and every fast food restaurant in your vicinity.

Now pull down the menu and let's see what's for lunch. Hit *CALCULATOR,* and Burger™ calculates the total bill for your lunch selection, transposing confusing foreign currencies into dollars and cents.

Daily and weekly calendars allow you to enter future lunch appointments. *Meet Rick Wolff at McDonald's, Istanbul, Turkey, March 18, 2084.* You can enter meal appointments in Burger™ for up to 850 years in advance of the present date.

Grease-retardant finish keeps Burger™ looking good meal after meal.

Taco?

Optional software cards expand Burger™'s powers. The Taco Card™ with 64 megabytes of ROM provides all of the same functions as Burger™, but for fast-food tacos, burritos, and fajitas. With Pizza Card™ you'll get a piping hot pizza delivered to your door—anywhere in the Milky Way.

- **Burger**™ (128 MB) #BURG128 **$499.95 (5.50)**
- **Styrofoam Carry Case** #RPOFF128 **$9.95 (2.00)**

BURGER SOFTWARE CARDS:

- **Taco Card**™ #BURGTAC64 **$129.95 (3.00)**
- **Pizza Card**™ #BURGPIZ64 **$119.95 (3.00)**

To order, call for pizza, no anchovies, then dial

1-800-UNEED-THIS

LET'S DO LUNCH

STEAL
WITH
STYLE
If you must steal, do it in style.
Just because no one should know your identity doesn't mean you shouldn't look your best. Our Face Stocking™ hosiery is constructed of the finest French sheer black nylon available. You'll love the comfortable, form-fitting stretch nylon, and with the high-density double-stitched design you can steal in full confidence, knowing that no one can get a positive ID. Best of all, you'll find that our Face Stocking™ breathes comfortably and effortlessly—an important feature you'll appreciate when you have the hose in place over your mouth and nose!
Our Face Stocking™ hosiery also includes several important features not commonly found in traditional hose: our hose will look fresh and wrinkle free, even after long hours in your back pocket. And it is guaranteed to ignite and burn completely in under three seconds, for quick disposal when you don't have time to wait.
Whether you're on a Paris fashion runway or in an alley on a getaway, look your absolute best with Face Stocking™. Why not commit your next felony in lace? Order today.
Now you can also order our exclusive Lace Gloves, and keep your fingerprints to yourself.
■ Face Stocking™ #DNTGO2JAIL $15.95 (2.50)
■ Lace Gloves #NOPRNTSNOWHRE $9.95 (2.50)
To order, holler loud into the phone
1-800-ECHO-ECHO

El Ledo.™ The Cadillac of lead-based writing instruments.

When Frank Lloyd Wright was sketching the design for the Falling Waters house, do you think he used the first pencil he could find? Of course not. And when JFK wrote ***Profiles in Courage***, what pencil did he use? The first number two he came across? Certainly not. Both Frank Lloyd Wright and JFK used an El Ledo™— the lead-based writing instrument from which greatness flows.

When you place an El Ledo™ in your hand, her heft and solid feel tell you instinctively that you've got your fingers wrapped around something very special. But the proof is in the writing. Note the way El Ledo™ accurately and effortlessly tracks across the page—almost like it *wants to write*. Note the excellent definition and sharpness, and the way El Ledo™ seems to magically maintain a sharp, geometrically perfect point.

Each El Ledo™ is equipped with a top-mounted erasure unit, constructed of a durable red polymer conglomerate. If you ever make a mistake while using El Ledo™, simply flip El Ledo™ over and lightly brush the erase feature across your error. Almost instantly, your mistakes vanish.

El Ledo™ comes with its own handsome calfskin leather case, with velvet and cashmere lining, along with a unique identifying number, and is personally signed by the craftsman who created it.

■ **El Ledo**™ #2PNCL **$22.95 (2.50)**

Let us put the jolt back in your java with our Super-Caffeinated Coffee.

If you're like us, and you drink a lot of coffee— say twenty to thirty cups a day or more—you know that sometimes you just don't get the caffeine "kick" that you're so accustomed to. One gulp of our super-caffeinated brew, though, and you'll immediately recognize that old familiar wake-up call, right on down to the sweaty palms, jittery fingers, and those good old caffeine twitches.

Our secret beans are grown on remote Mt. Semeru on the Indonesian island of Java. Here, highly energized natives work twenty-hour days, six and seven days a week, throughout the year, cultivating their super-caffeinated beans.

Our secret blend is *not* approved for sale as a food under present FDA guidelines. Every order must be accompanied by a written prescription from your doctor. May cause extreme tachycardia, faintness, or outright panic in some users.

■ **Super-Caffeinated Coffee (1 lb.) #HITEST $19.95 (3.00)**

Post Race.™ The *after-race* horse race analyzer.

Post Race™ is the first horse race analyzer designed to be used *after the race is over!*

Here's how this revolutionary new gaming device works: once the race is over, find a discarded ticket. Any ticket. Then use the soft-touch, beverage-resistant key pad to enter the track name and date, race number, horse number, bet (win, place or show), and the amount shown on the face of the ticket. Don't worry if you come across an unclaimed ticket that's a few months old—Post Race™ comes preprogrammed with the results for every horse race in the United States, from 1909 through to the date of purchase of your unit. Once you've entered your ticket information, Post Race™ then compares your ticket with its massive internal database. If you're in luck, Post Race™'s LCD screen flashes *YOU WIN!* while playing the theme from "A Day at the Races." If your discarded ticket is a dud, you'll see *TRY AGAIN.* The built-in calculator lets you tabulate your winnings.

Order Post Race™ today, and before you know it you'll be cleaning up at the track in more ways than one.

■ **Post Race Horse Race Analyzer**™
#FRTOTLOSRS **$199.95 (10.00)**

Climb high, real high, with the world's tallest ladder.

Stairway to Heaven Ladder™ features over *400* individual telescoping titanium-aluminum sections, giving you a whopping total of more than 9,000 feet of usable vertical ladder height. That's almost *two miles* of ladder!

And when you're two miles into space, you don't want to be hanging on to a piece of inferior craftsmanship. That's why each rung of this ladder is reinforced with construction-grade rebar, and includes a high-friction sure-grip rubber coating. Telescoping sections feature a quicklock, positive-action camming mechanism, virtually eliminating perilous section failures.

Don't let short ladders and step stools stop you from getting what you want in life. Order our Stairway to Heaven Ladder™ today!

■ **Stairway to Heaven Ladder**™
#DNTLKDWN **$1,299.99 (250.00)**

Never use Stairway to Heaven Ladder™ near power lines or near FAA-approved approach patterns to major airports.

Big Chew Trophies.™ Start your collection today!

When you think of America's favorite pastime, what's the first thing that comes to mind? If you're like most Americans, chances are your answer is, "Guys chewing big wads of bubble gum." Sadly, until recently, those big wads were thoughtlessly discarded. Now, though, Big Chew Trophies™ brings the famous bubble gum wads of big league players right into your home.

Each Big Chew Trophy™ is certified to have spent at least three innings in the mouth of the all-star player of your choice, and is lacquered in the exact form it was ejected from the player's mouth. Trophies are available from Don Mattingly, Roger Clemens, Jose Canseco, Nolan Ryan, and Kirby Puckett. Look for more Big Chew Trophies™ coming soon!

Order three or more Big Chew Trophies™ now and receive a free mystery vial of tobacco juice from an up-and-coming AAA league player.

■ **Big Chew Trophies**™ (Specify Player) #WADOCHW **$69.95 (5.00)**

Burnt Toast extends your life for ten, twenty, thirty years or more.

The Cutting Edge is thrilled to offer burnt toast. Why burnt toast? Because it will actually prolong your life, thanks to the discovery of the unusual enzyme, Life+™.

Life+™ was discovered by scientists at the Massachusetts Institute of Technology's new George Burns Center for Applied Geriatric Research. For years, researchers postulated that yogurt was responsible for the impressive longevity of the indigenous population living in the Ural mountains. But yogurt had nothing to do with it! Rather, it was Life+™, a rare enzyme created when bread particles are scorched. When taken into the body via a toast "vehicle," Life+™ is absorbed into the blood stream and acts to soothe the hypothalamus, the body's regulatory center for growth and aging. Thanks to the searing hot, coal-fired campfires and their toast-intensive diet, these peasants were ingesting enough Life+™ to keep them going for centuries!

A toast—for life!

How much burnt toast is right for you? Check the Life+™ Chart below before ordering. (One Order of Burnt Toast is two slices of toast.) While the USRDA has yet to be established for Life+™, this chart is based upon the dosage suggested by the chemical industry's Center for the Advancement of Life+™.

- **One Order Burnt Toast, White** #CRBNPELETWHT **$10.95 (2.50)**
- **One Order Burnt Toast, Wheat** #CRBNPELETWHE **$10.95 (2.50)**

DETERMINE YOUR RECOMMENDED DAILY DOSAGE OF SLICES OF BURNT TOAST BY REFERRING TO THIS EASY TO USE CHART:

DESIRED LIFE EXPECTANCY	100	125	150	OVER 150
PRESENT AGE				
Under 30	1	2	5	8
31-50	2	3	8	12
51-70	8	12	30	75
71-90	10	16	50	105
Over 91	25	55	205	8,075

To order, call for pizza, no anchovies, then dial

1-800-UNEED-THIS

Who would own luggage that looks like this?

Practically no one. And that's good news for you, because with Yamani's new Happy Face Luggage, you'll always know which bag is yours the moment it hits the carousel.

Luxurious Venezuelan calfskin. And a big happy face!

Each piece of Happy Face Luggage is handcrafted from top quality Venezuelan calfskin, and features reinforced double-stitched seams. The platinum-plated YKK zipper is oversized, which virtually assures you you'll never have to endure another embarrassing zipper "blow-out."

Yamani's reputation for attention to detail is evident throughout the Happy Face series, right down to the bright banana yellow happy face. Each happy face is constructed from rugged 2000-denier, rip-stop nylon and is attached with an epoxy-strength industrial sealant, then bar tacked and seam sealed to the luggage.

Yamani's five-piece Happy Face series can be purchased together or separately. If ordering separately, please specify Happy Garment Carrier, Happy Pullman, Happy Carry-On or Happy Weekender.

Keep on smiling, because it's guaranteed.

Our Yamani Happy Face series comes with a unique "don't worry—be happy" guarantee: if anyone ever mistakes your luggage for their own, we'll replace the contents of your lost Happy Face bag at no cost to you. And to further assure against that ever happening, Yamani has made a solemn pledge not to sell more than one Happy Face bag per 1,000 people. Once this Happy Face Luggage level of market penetration has been reached, no additional bags will be sold. Period.

Be happy. Order your very own set of Yamani Happy Face Luggage today.

HAPPY FACE LUGGAGE

Item	Number	Price	
■ **Complete Happy Set**	#OHSOHPY	**$1,195.00**	**(35.00)**
■ **Happy Garment**	#HPYGAR	**$ 399.00**	**(15.00)**
■ **Happy Pullman**	#HPYPUL	**$ 299.00**	**(10.00)**
■ **Happy Carry-On**	#HPYCAR	**$ 199.00**	**(8.00)**
■ **Happy Weekender**	#THNKGDITSFRI	**$ 299.00**	**(10.00)**

"Air travel is no problem with my new Happy Face Luggage. I used to misplace and mistake bags all the time. Now it never happens. Thanks, Yamani!"
—Frequent flyer and ABC news foreign correspondent Pierre Salinger

These shoes will last a lifetime. Or two.

From "The Pump" to the "Energy Return System," every year the major shoe companies have a new gimmick to offer. But in a remote corner of Sicily, the Carlione family has quietly been constructing some of the finest and most durable footwear in the world for more than four decades.

It all began at the end of World War II, when Cementos™ founder Giuseppe Carlione accidentally stepped in a bucket of wet concrete while rebuilding his family's home. Working alone, his shouts of "Mamma mia, sono incastrato nel cemento!" went unanswered. The concrete dried—and, much to his surprise, Giuseppe just loved the results. You will too.

As durable as a parking garage.

Cementos™ incorporate everything you've always wanted in a shoe—fashion, comfort, and, most of all, durability. Serious durability. Because each pair of Cementos™ is handcrafted from grade 5, impermeable Italian foundation-quality cement, the finest cement available at any price. On the inside, Carlione structural engineers have incorporated a series of steel I-beams encased in a rugged synthetic polymer, making certain that Cementos™ will maintain their structural integrity for years to come. Plus, Cementos™ are comfortable—so comfortable, in fact, that they're the only shoes ever to receive the enthusiastic endorsement of both the American Podiatric Medical Association *and* the American Society of Civil Engineers.

Now available in five great styles.

Cementos™ are available in five great styles, including the executive style Cemento Alphonso™, Cemento Vino™ for the night life, the Signorina Carlione™ for the ladies, Cemento Bambino™ for the little ones, and the rugged Cemento Macho™ for the active outdoors lifestyle. Whatever style you chose, though, we're certain you'll be glad you cleared a spot in your garage for a pair of Cementos™.

After your shoes have passed the rugged chip and drop tests performed on all Cementos™, they will be issued a Cemento Certificate of Occupancy and shipped directly to you.

■ **Cemento Alphonso™**	#CNCRTEXEC	**$225.00**	**(55.00)**
■ **Cemento Vino™**	#CNCRTEVE	**$225.00**	**(55.00)**
■ **Signorina Carlione™**	#LITLLDYCNCRT	**$225.00**	**(55.00)**
■ **Cemento Macho™**	#CONCRTMACHO	**$250.00**	**(65.00)**
■ **Cemento Bambino™**	#CNCRTBABY	**$150.00**	**(45.00)**

Please indicate size when ordering.
Sorry, Cementos™ cannot be poured in half-sizes.

To order, sing *"New York, New York"* ten times and call:

1-800-DO-BE-DO-BE-DO

The Cutting Edge recommends periodic resealing of Cementos™ with Thompson's Water Seal.

Executive Style
Cemento Alphonso™

HIT THE ROAD, JACK

YOU NEED TO BUY SOME MORE THINGS TODAY!

Approximately 30% of all calls placed will result in wrong numbers. Please note that some dead persons refuse to return calls.

Direct line to the dead features auto redial, speaker phone, and 10-memory dialing.

Just because an associate, relative, or loved one is dead, doesn't mean you shouldn't *reach out and touch them.* Some of the best business and personal advice comes from colleagues who have lived a long and fulfilling life—exactly the sort of people who are most frequently dead *and* the most difficult to get ahold of. With Dead Phone™ you can talk to these people—for as long as you like. They have nothing but time.

How does this high-tech cellular phone from Dearly Beloved Technologies, Inc. cross the ether? We're not quite certain. And no one on the other end will tell us, either. It appears, however, that the cellular phone is acting as a channeling medium—a regular high-tech interface between Heaven and Earth. All you have to do is place the *DEAD RECEPTOR™* up against an article of clothing, or anything else belonging to the deceased, or hold it up to his or her picture. Then just wait for a dial tone and dial their number. We can't yet promise the crystal-clear reception of a fiber optics network, but if you listen closely and block out the inter-world static, you'll soon be talking with all your dead friends.

And there's no charge—yet.

Best of all, calling a dead person doesn't cost a cent. There are no local network charges, no long distance carrier charges—nothing! Dead Phone™ users of several years report that they have yet to receive a bill on their regular phone bill, or separate billing from *anywhere* or *anyone.* Other than the price of the phone, the only additional charge you pay is a one-time hook up charge of $150.00, paid directly to The Cutting Edge.

Did you know that when friends and colleagues die, many times their phone numbers change? Not sure just what number to dial? Order our optional Dead Yellow Pages.

■ **Dead Phone™**	#DEDPHNE	**$595.95 (10.00)**
■ **Dead Yellow Pages** (Please Specify Year)	#DEDPAGE	**$55.95 (10.00)**

These headstones have a lot to say.

What better way for your loved ones to remember you by, than an attractive, animated Talking Headstone™ from Dearly Beloved Technologies, Inc., the makers of our popular Dead Phone™.

Six feet under—and *still* getting in the last word!

Did friends use to call you "unstoppable?" Now you can prove them right, for eternity!

Imagine having friends and family coming to visit your grave—and you're "your old self"—full of lively conversation, witty comebacks, and snappy one liners—that same "joie de vivre" that you used to have, until you died. And because a Talking Headstone™ turns a visit to your graveside from a somber, depressing experience into an enjoyable outing for friends and relatives, this headstone is an exceptionally thoughtful way to show your consideration and caring towards others.

A headstone that's a dead ringer for the old you.

Send us a photo of yourself, as you look now or as you would like to be remembered, and the master sculptors at Dearly Beloved Technologies, Inc. will create, in loving detail, your own personal talking gravestone that is a *dead ringer* for the old you. Your Talking Headstone™ is hand sculpted from the very same durable, flesh-like plastic that's used in Hollywood special effects studios. So lifelike, friends and family will have a hard time believing that they aren't actually talking to the real thing.

Your Talking Headstone™ uses two tiny microphones, embedded in each ear, to accurately identify up to 50 different, preprogrammed visitor voices. When a voice is detected and its speaker is identified, your Talking Headstone™ will respond with one of more than 300 preselected expressions. (Before you go to the great beyond, please send us a cassette with your favorite lines and repartees recorded for all possible graveside visitors.) Because your Talking Headstone™ receives its power from a miniature solar array mounted on the rear of its head, there's no need to count on unreliable relatives to constantly change batteries.

Talking Headstone™. A Cutting Edge exclusive.

- **Talking Headstone**™ (One Head)
  #1DEDHED **$495.00 (45.00)**
- **Talking Headstones**™ (Two Heads)
  #2DEDHEDS **$895.00 (65.00)**

Protect your important computer files with the explosive power of TNT.

If computer security is a problem for you, we have the solution. Restrict access to your files with five construction-grade sticks of good old-fashioned dynamite.

MacBoomBoom™ uses five, three-pound sticks of dynamite, made from the highest quality nitroglycerine and ammonium nitrate. When an incorrect password is entered into your computer, a high-voltage pulse is transmitted from the MacBoomBoom Sentry Circuit™ to the explosive charge, instantaneously detonating all five sticks of dynamite.

How powerful is a five stick dynamite charge? Here's one example: one fifth of one stick of dynamite is enough to completely disintegrate a TV-sized boulder into individual pieces no bigger than a peanut. Let's just say that being "blown to kingdom come" is an *understatement* for what will happen to whoever tries to access your files next time.

MacBoomBoom™. It may not be pretty, but it's effective.

■ **MacBoomBoom™** #MACSMTHRENS **$99.95 (25.00)**

MacBoomBoom™ users are encouraged to back up their hard disks daily. The Cutting Edge is not responsible for home or office cleanup after detonation of MacBoomBoom™.

FOR THE T

PARAN

*Please remember that if you have the **slightest** doubt remembering your password, do not attempt to access your computer.*

To order, seek professional help, then call

1-800-I-DONT-GET-IT

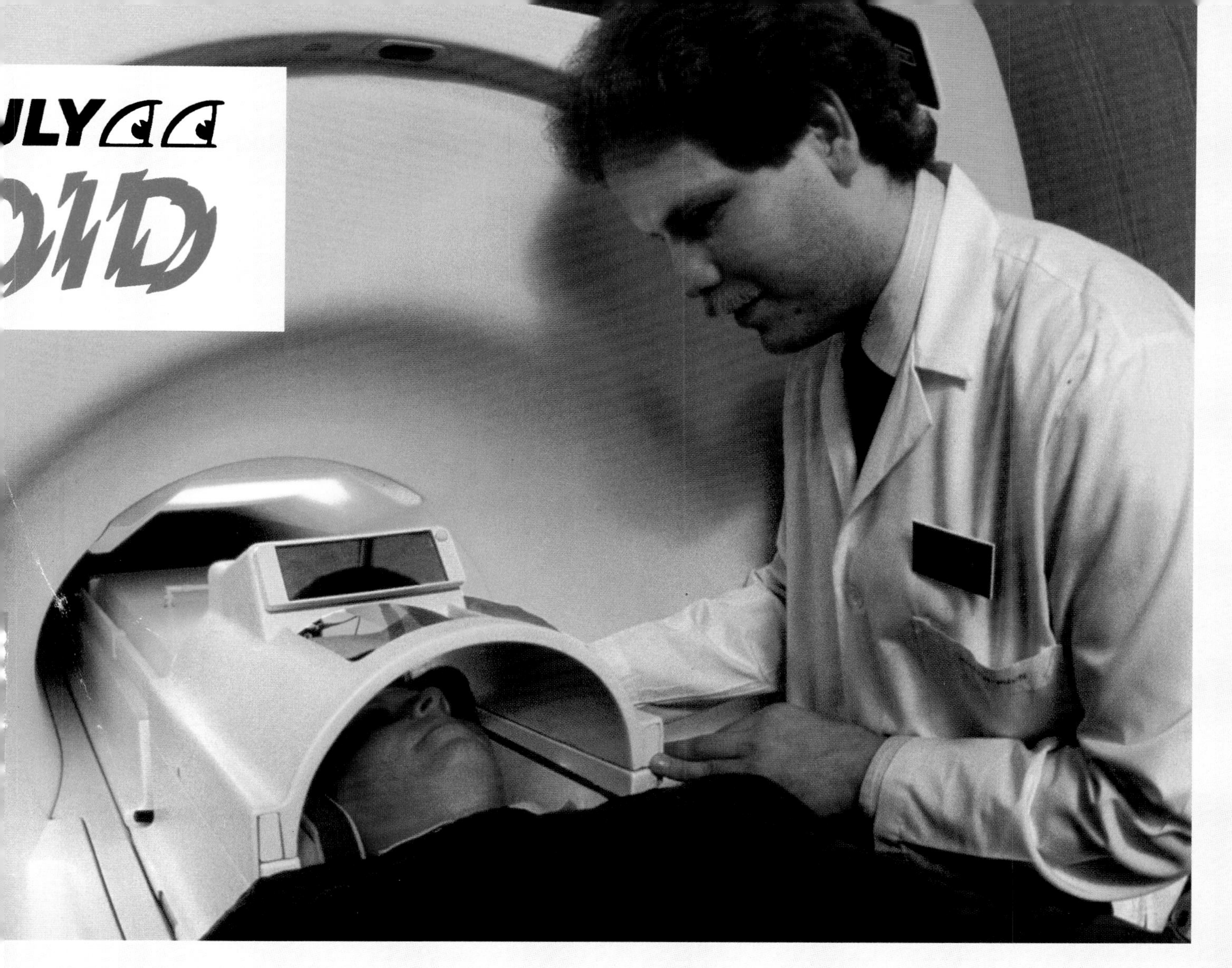

"Was I adopted?" Find out once and for all with ScanMan.™

For too many of us, those words haunt us day to day. They keep us awake at night, and they distract us during our every waking hour.

Did you know that over 80% of children who were adopted were lied to by their adopted parents? It's a fact. So you can never really be sure. Until now.

Get the DNA truth from your supposed "parents."

The principle behind ScanMan™ is simple. As you and your "parents" relax in your individual scanning modules, ScanMan™ bombards your body with high levels of non-ionizing radiation. Powerful diagnostic scanners digitally compare your DNA with the DNA of your purported "parents." Since each person has a unique DNA "ID" derived from his or her parents, ScanMan™'s results are guaranteed 100% accurate. When the thirty-minute scan is complete, just step over to the control unit and check the display panel. A "match" indicates that your true parents were in the ScanMan™ unit with you, while "match mother, no match father," "match father, no match mother," or "no match, no match" indicates that you still haven't been told the full story.

A mix up in maternity?

ScanMan™ can also be used by parents to confirm that "their" child is actually their biological child. The fact is, accidental swapping of babies in the maternity ward is much more common than many hospitals admit. If you have the slightest thought that junior doesn't really look all that much like mom and dad, perhaps it's time you scanned the whole family.

Who can put a price on "peace of mind"?

We can. And advanced medical technology like ScanMan™ doesn't come cheap. But if you're losing valuable time wondering *"was I adopted?"* or if you're spending thousands of dollars on daily psychoanalysis, you'll find that even at $775,000.00, ScanMan™ will actually *save you money*.

Don't let this debilitating psychological worry slow you down in life. Order ScanMan™ today, and tomorrow you'll know whether to call that woman with the familiar, smiling face "Mom"—or by some other name.

■ **ScanMan™**
#OHNO!IMADOPTED **$775,000.00 (5,000.00)**

Sorry, delivery not available.

"Who said that about me?!?" Now you can know for sure, with your own personal satellite.

Is someone talking about you behind your back? Chances are very good the answer is "yes!" And if you're a corporate decision maker, or tend to have an active social life, studies show there's a better than fifty-fifty chance that someone is talking about you *right now*. With odds like this, it's important to take preventive measures to protect yourself from damaging rumors and innuendo.

Our new Personal Geosynchronous Satellite is a genuine, fully functional orbiting satellite that monitors everything that is said within its 3,500-square-mile coverage pattern. Highly selective circuitry filters out millions of conversations, focusing in on and amplifying only those conversations that are about you. When someone says something about you, your satellite alerts you via a convenient pager unit. Coordinates are displayed, showing the location of the conversation to within fifty feet, and a display light flashes every time your name is mentioned. (Called by more than one pleasant or unpleasant nickname? Don't worry—your satellite can accept up to thirty names or name variations.) Order the optional BigEars™ module if you would like to *actually listen in* on the conversation.

Your Personal Geosynchronous Satellite will be carried into space aboard NASA's Endeavor space shuttle. Due to launch backlog, please allow three to four years from date of order for your satellite to be placed in its designated orbital slot.

- **Personal Geosynchronous Satellite**
  #WHOSADTHTBOUTME? **$195,000.00 (535,000.00)**
- **BigEars™ Audio Option**
  #IHERDTHAT! **$30,000.00 (FREE!)**

Shipping price increases are beyond the control of The Cutting Edge.

Sorry, delivery and gift wrapping not available.

Get a jump on the Big One. With LastCall.™

No one likes to plan for the prospect of a nuclear war. Why, that's as bad as having to see the dentist! Still, the threat of nuclear annihilation won't go away on its own—and that's why we all need LastCall™.

When a few minutes can mean a lifetime.

With LastCall™, you'll be alerted to a nuclear strike up to *fifteen minutes* before the national emergency broadcast system transmits its first tones. This nifty little device senses the electromagnetic wave disruption that typically occurs in the ionosphere just moments prior to a nuclear release. As soon as an ionospheric disturbance is detected, LastCall™ emits an attention getting 150-decibel, 1-kilohertz tone that's audible for nearly two miles. A built-in meter indicates the severity of attack— *ONE* is a relatively minor attack of under 10 kilotons, *TEN* is a full-scale superpower level nuclear attack with equivalent explosive power of several hundred megatons of weaponry.

When several hundred nuclear-tipped warheads are headed towards your city, wouldn't it be nice to have a little advance warning? Give your loved ones those extra precious moments together that they'll appreciate for a lifetime to come. Give them LastCall™.

- **LastCall™** #BEEPBEEP-KABOOM! **$199.95 (7.50)**

LastCall™ may accidentally be set off by microwave oven use, amateur radio transmitters, or your TV remote controller.

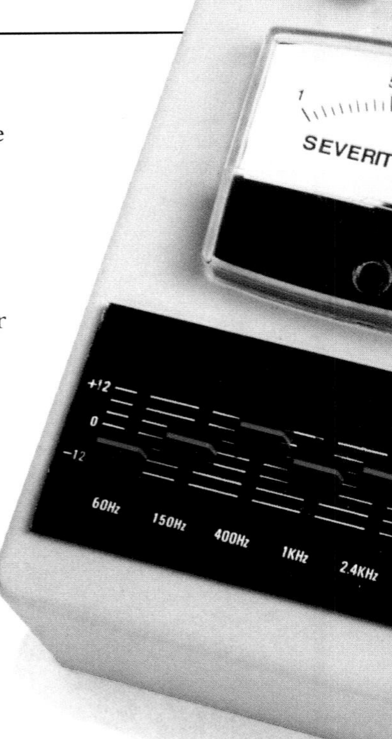

Exercise safely with CycleAlert.™

Did you know that nearly 30% of all fatal heart attacks occur while using an aerobic exercise device, such as a bicycle, treadmill, or stairclimber? That's why you want to approach your workout with the utmost care—to assure that it won't be your last.

CycleAlert™ is the only stationary bike available that keeps tabs on all the parameters of your body's three primary life systems: pulmonary oxygen exchange, heart function, and systolic blood pressure. Pulmonary oxygen levels are monitored via a two-way, nonrebreather mouthpiece, while heart function is closely monitored via six reusable, adhesive epidermal electrodes. Blood pressure sensing requires placement of a subvenous wide-bore catheter in either arm.

Once all three sensors are in place, just enter your weight, age, and sex, mount the cycle unit, and go to it. If anything ever goes wrong, you'll be the first to know. A front-mounted, five-inch speaker announces your physiological status in a calm, reassuring voice. And with more than one hundred announcements, ranging from "status healthy—continue exercise" to "please rest—respiratory status questionable," right on through to the big one, "stop immediately—ventricular fibrillation in progress!," you'll be on top of your health every moment. If CycleAlert™ senses one of thirty-five life-threatening conditions, your exercise pedals will automatically lock in place to prevent further exercise.

Now everyone can enjoy a good, long, *safe* workout. Cycle smart, with CycleAlert™.

■ **CycleAlert**™ #PRNOIDSWET **$899.95 (65.00)**

CycleAlert™ may not detect all forms of arrhythmia or myocardial infarction of the left atrium. Persons with a family history of heart disease should not operate CycleAlert™ without having immediate access to defibrillator paddles.

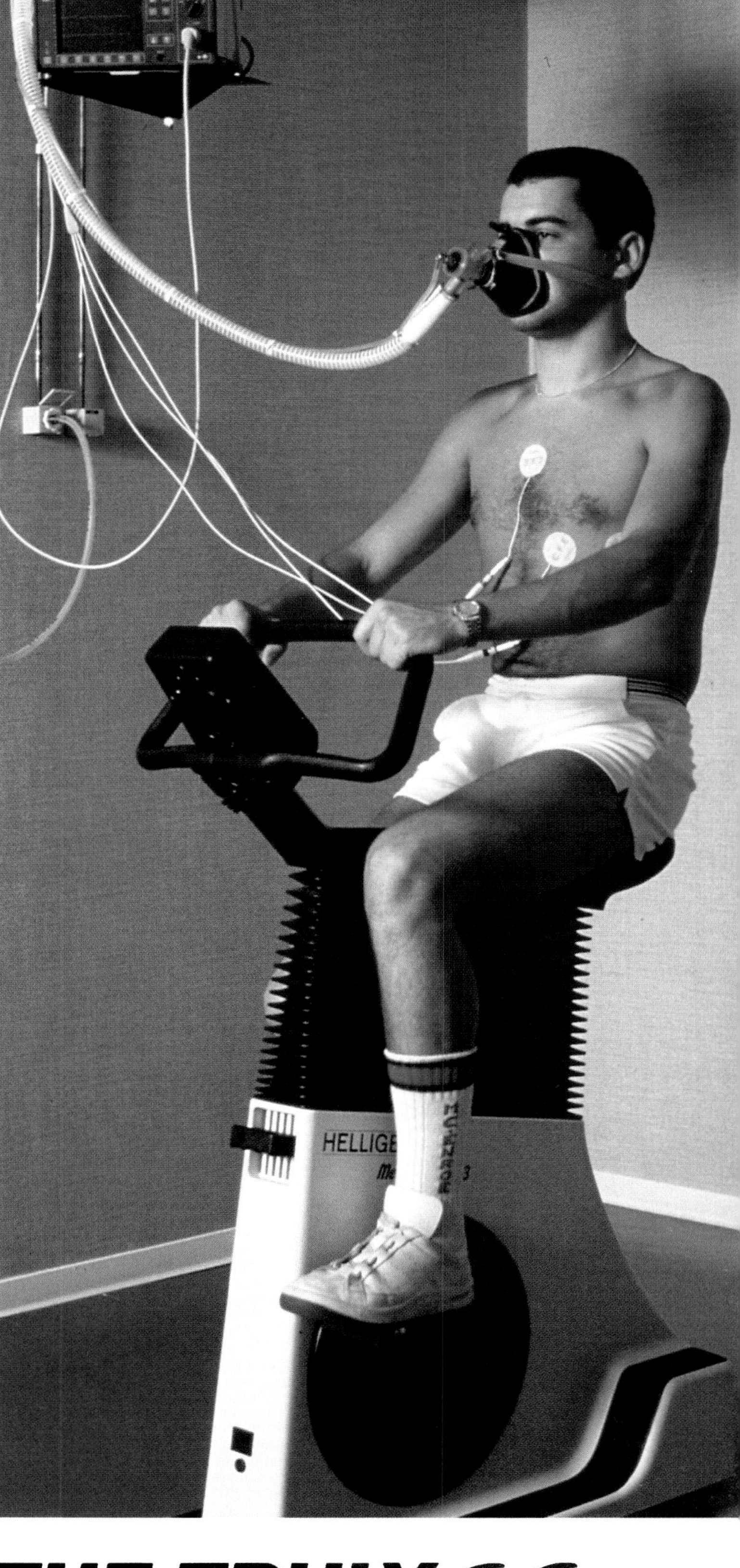

To order, scan line for wire taps and call

1-800-WHYME

INCREASE YOUR CREDIT CARD LIMIT. ASK US HOW.

FOR THE TRULY PARANOID

Housemaster Homes.™ The final word in home exercise.

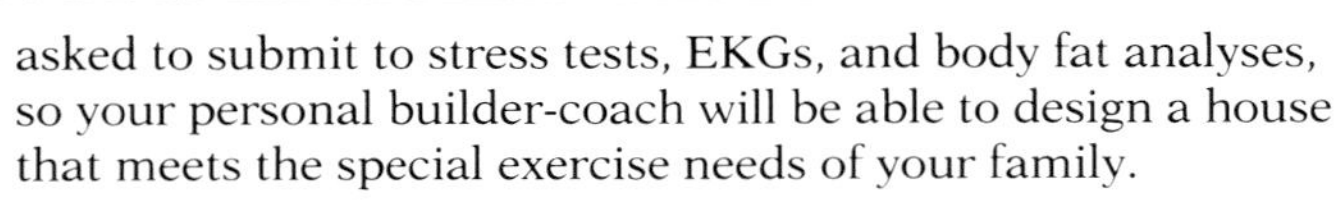

Home exercise takes on a whole new meaning with Housemaster Homes™, the final word in home exercise. *Housemaster™ is the only house in the world that is specifically and completely designed from the ground up with your exercise in mind.*

If you choose to live in a Housemaster Home™, you'll begin your odyssey by first meeting with your family's personal builder-coach. Each member of the family will be asked to submit to stress tests, EKGs, and body fat analyses, so your personal builder-coach will be able to design a house that meets the special exercise needs of your family.

Burn three hundred calories just opening a window!

No pain no gain—*24 hours a day.*

Living in a Housemaster Home™ is no picnic. Imagine—a bedroom door that won't open without a 200-pound manual squat thrust, or a rotating staircase that demands a five-minute sprint to reach the second floor, or even a static-charged high-friction plush carpet that requires super strong calves to negotiate. In your new home, even the most minor activity will burn hundreds of calories and build muscle. Common, repetitive motions, such as turning on lights or opening drawers, are designed to build aerobic muscle endurance, while infrequent activities, such as opening the garage door or unscrewing light bulbs, work to build anaerobic muscle bulk.

Each and every exercise unit in a Housemaster Home™ includes a specially designed "reset to zero" feature. If you don't complete the task in the allocated, preprogrammed time, you will be required to start over. For example, if you do not reach the second floor in under thirty seconds, your rotating staircase will speedily deposit you back on the first floor. After a brief rest, you may try again.

Housemaster™ knows all.

Thanks to hundreds of pressure sensitive sensors built into your home's floor, your Housemaster Home™ "knows" the location of each member of your family, at any given moment. What does this mean for you? It means that every one of the more than 1,000 exercise devices, from doorknobs to windowsills to friction carpets, is constantly adjusted to meet the specific needs of each member of the family, from grandpa right on through to the family dog.

Opening a Housemaster™ garage door is equivalent to bench pressing 175 pounds.

Sorry, not included.

Out of shape relatives coming to visit?

Your 4,000-square-foot Housemaster Home™ is designed with you in mind. For example, the designers of Housemaster™ know that every now and then your new home may prove to be just a little too tiring, a little too demanding. That's why each Housemaster Home™ comes equipped with a 100-square-foot "safe harbor" room, where you can relax without fear of confronting yet another exercise device. Plus, each year your designated Houseleader™ is allowed to preset up to ten "rest days" for your family and an additional seven "holiday" events per year, during which Housemaster™ will negate all exercise functions, for the benefit of out of shape, visiting friends and relatives. If not for this unique feature, old Uncle Ed might never leave your "safe harbor" room— all Christmas day!

Are you up to the Housemaster™ challenge?

Living in a Housemaster Home™ isn't for everyone. Some home owners will choose to move back to a more traditional, sedentary style of living. However, if you stick with it, we're confident you'll come to love the only house ever endorsed by the President's Commission on Physical Fitness.

Call us today for a free, initial appointment with your personal builder-coach.

- **Housemaster Homes™ are available in Contemporary, Tudor, Victorian, and Ranch styles.**
  #PNINTHEBT **Prices start at $499,000.00**

Only the man in the house can lift this toilet seat!

A beautiful Housemaster Home™, Contemporary style.

To order, call while bungee cord jumping

1-800-BE-BOP-A-LU-LA

Calories Burned During Home Exercise

Conventional Home	**Housemaster Home™**
Opening Front Door: 10	With Housemaster Thrust-a-Door™: 300
Lifting Toilet Lid: 10	With Housemaster Lidmaster™: 200-500
Making Breakfast: 200	With Housemaster PowerKitchen™: 2,500-5,000
Going up One Flight of Stairs: 50	With Housemaster Roto-Flight™: 400-600
Vacuuming Living Room Carpet: 100	With Housemaster FrictionCarpet™: 800-1,200

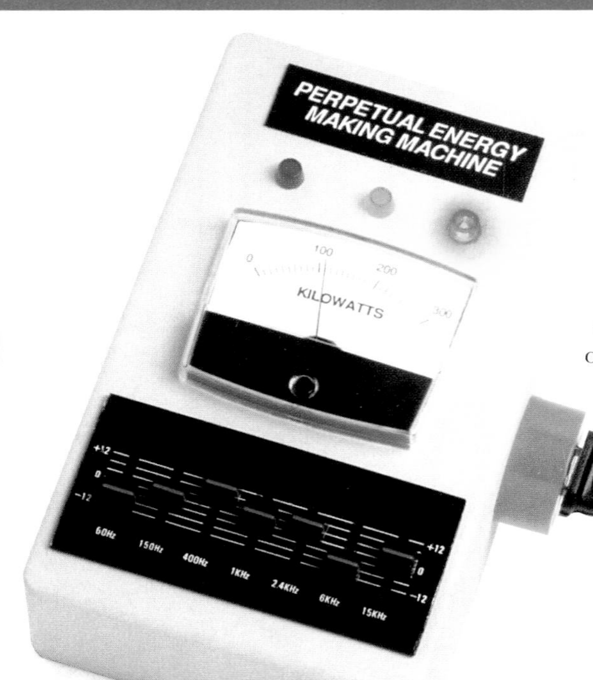

Unlimited energy. Forever. For free.

Imagine for a moment that every home and every office suddenly had an unlimited, clean, and inexhaustible source of power. An unobtainable Utopia? We thought so. Until we came across MegaTech's Perpetual Energy Making Machine — made in the land of the Rising Sun.

Imagine — more than one hundred kilowatts of clean, regulated alternating current are available on a continual basis through the 120 volt AC outlet located on its side panel! You will delight as you watch your energy meter swing to the right while you draw on your unlimited supply of electrical power.

The Perpetual Energy Making Machine has no moving parts, requires no maintenance, and is not user serviceable.

Order one unit for small to medium homes, two units for larger homes and offices, and "get off the grid" for good.

A Cutting Edge exclusive.

■ **Perpetual Energy Making Machine**
#BALONEY ~~$199.95~~ $149.95 (7.50)

WHY ORDER JUST ONE, WHEN YOU CAN ORDER TWO OR THREE?

ON SALE!

Statues of the Gods. Bring a little B.C. into your home today.

Imagine having a rare, twenty-foot high religious icon that's over *two thousand* years old, standing solemnly in your living room. Only famous-name museums could afford such a work, right? Wrong! Working with the archeology departments of leading universities and several third-world leaders, The Cutting Edge is able to offer these religious icons to the general public for a nominal price.

Handcrafted by ancient sculptors for important religious events, these Statues of the Gods are carved from durable indigenous stone and feature dramatic facial expressions. And, because our research shows that each craftsman was sacrificed once his statue was completed, we can assure you that no two Statues of the Gods are exactly alike.

Order now, as these Statues of the Gods are in very limited supply. The Cutting Edge is not responsible for chips, cracks, or fissures. All statues sold "as is." Absolutely no refunds or exchanges.

■ **Statue of the Gods**
#SMUGGLDOUT
~~$1,750.00~~ $199.95 (995.00)

Please note that your Statue of the God will arrive via land freight, carefully boxed in a carton labelled "International Relief Supplies — Do Not Inspect". *The Cutting Edge cannot provide information on the country of origin of your Statue of the God.*